Help! I'm in Love!

the dynamics of e-motion

Emmanuel Osana-Isaac

WestBow
PRESS
A DIVISION OF THOMAS NELSON

ISBN: 978-1-4497-6633-7 (sc)
ISBN: 978-1-4497-6635-1 (e)
ISBN: 978-1-4497-6634-4 (hc)
WestBow Press books may be ordered through booksellers or by contacting:
WestBow Press
A Division of Thomas Nelson
1663 Liberty Drive
Bloomington, IN 47403
www.westbowpress.com
1-(866) 928-1240

Library of Congress Control Number: 2012916730
Printed in the United States of America
WestBow Press rev. date: 9/17//2012

Contents

To Divyne, who has taught me what it means to love and be loved.

Love is a verb, not a noun. It is not just something you feel, but something you do!

Preface

O ur lives have been preset. We are born, we attend school, we graduate, we get a job, and then we get married. Everyone born into this world follows the same script as written by culture and society. Life is *spent* chasing the dream of happiness as described by the prevailing circumstances. Along the line of spending our lives, we discover that some commodities are more expensive than others; we discover that there are rules in the marketplace that nobody bothered to teach us.

Love as a commodity in the market of life has been severely abused. Every young man and woman goes into the market in search of love. Their intention is to leave the market only after they have *found* love. The challenge most of the time, though, is that they would not recognize love even if it was right in front of them. They have never learned about it. A lot of them go into the market oblivious of the price of love and unaware of the twists and turns around the road. Many have said that it is something you fall into. They say they *fell* in love. Others say it's something they can make. They claim to have a plant that produces love. They usually describe their sexual encounters as *making love*. All in a bid to help others recognize it when they see it, they describe love in all sorts of ways. They say it is blind; others claim it is wicked; some even go ahead to say it feels like butterflies in the tummy. A lot of people leave the market without finding what they went in to get *due* to this gross misunderstanding; others leave more confused than ever, even concluding that love is a mirage. A lucky few find it but discover that they know nothing about it. So their lives become a lab experiment of love; they spend life searching for the appropriate manual to teach them how to operate their new device.

In your hands right now is one such manual that promises to show you in glaring pictures what exactly to search for in the market. For those lucky few who have actually found it already, this book points you in the right direction, showing how to carefully fit the parts of your *love device* together.

I have changed the names in all the stories you will see in this book to protect the identities of the persons concerned. Additionally, several of the stories are the author's own adaptations of the true events as recorded in the Bible.

Acknowledgments

First of all, I give all the glory and praise to God for the inspiration and ability to put these truths to paper. If it were not for his constant pulls and prods, there would be nothing here.

Also, I'm grateful to all the people that have helped in reading and rereading the manuscripts and suggesting changes. Without them, there would be no success. I especially want to thank Divyne, Dammy and Busola Metibemu, Toluwalase, Isaac Osana, Omoh Osagie, and Lisa Nurmilaukas. They did a lot of encouraging and reading to help turn the manuscript into a book worth reading.

I would also love to thank all the people who gave me permission to publish their stories in this book, and all those who supported this project in one way or the other. You have joined the wagon of people using their lives to change lives.

I am greatly indebted to Divyne, the love of my life. Many of the things I know I learned from her. She is the "engine of this car."

Finally, I want to thank my parents. They have shown me that love can weather the storms of life.

Milling the Mile

With the rise in rates of divorce and the collapse of the family, one is forced to ask if love has gone on vacation. Everyone claims to be in love, but all the mess still happens.

The couple that divorced down the street once claimed to be in love with each other.

The guy that hit his wife once claimed he loved her.

The woman that cheated on her husband once said she loved him.

The questions I keep asking are these: "Where is the love? What happened to it?"

The question many people need to ask themselves is this: "Am I really in love?"

This very pertinent question arose in a discussion I had with a friend some time ago. We were discussing issues that were pertinent to our lives, and along the way, we delved into marriages and relationships—of course the discussion would not have been complete without it! We began to share experiences—ours and friends'—that we considered important. We talked about the problems that abound in homes and budding relationships; we wondered why love has become synonymous to sex; we wondered why it was becoming increasingly difficult for people, especially young Christians, to keep themselves till marriage. Although I thought I had the answers, I subsequently discovered that sincerity is quite different from arrogance! We concluded that day by agreeing to go home with this question. We also decided that we would sincerely answer this question to ourselves.

The process of answering these questions was very revealing. I got home that night, lay on my bed, and called God to invigilate the examination—self-examination—I was about to take.

That night, I began to understand that there are several forces at play in every man and woman. The events that unfolded in the days that followed taught me that it is one thing to know what you want to do, and it is another thing to do what you want to do. I began to understand that it is one thing to set boundaries; it is another thing to keep them. I discovered that we have misunderstood love; we have refused to understand how it works. We do not know how love grows and the attendant forces that accompany it. We think that merely saying, "I love you," insulates us from external pressures that bring shame and regret. I realized that it is folly to ignore and consider as unworthy the power that comes with emotions, especially when one is in love. I realized that emotions are so strong that they can make us do things we would never have imagined.

Let me explain what I mean with this short but true story.

I got a call from a friend of mine, Cynthia. She wanted to come over to my place. Of course, I had no problem with that—that's why we have a sitting room. When she arrived, we got to talking, talking about things in general. Then she began to tell me why she had come. She narrated a story that was nothing but heartrending. She told me how she had lost her virginity and how she climbed up the ladder to sexual orgies! Amidst tears, she said, "My life has not gone the way I planned it. I planned to get married as a virgin. Now look where I am!"

Now the question I asked Cynthia was, "What happened? Why did you let yourself degenerate?" The truth is that she planned, prayed, and wished to protect herself from premarital sex. Was that not enough?

There are many people like Cynthia who are born-again, tongue-talking, Spirit-filled brothers and sisters. They have made up their minds to be pure, but along the line, they end up where they did not plan. In my first year in the university, I boasted to my best friend. I said, "The Devil would be making the biggest mistake of his life if he decides to tempt me with ladies; he should know I will never fall." My friend replied, "Don't be so sure!" Of course, I did not want to agree with him openly, but I knew deep down my honest spine that he was dead correct! There are a lot of people like that who are boasting in their power and ability. I remained like that till the day I sincerely asked, "Am I really in love?" Asking and answering that question brought to the fore several factors that I and many others like me have either chosen to ignore or taken for granted!

What happens when a young man is friends with a young lady? What happens when a young man is in love with a young woman? What happens when a young lady is courting a young man? Obviously, nobody wants to talk about it. I am not talking about the dynamics of communication and love or mutual respect. I am talking about the high-tension wire of emotions! Let's not be too holy to admit it. It exists! Sadly, it takes control most of the times! During courtship, a lot of people lose it. They either become careless or too careful. Carelessness and over-carefulness are two evils that have destroyed the foundation of many a marriage. I'll illustrate with this story.

The Phillips are a family I have known since my childhood. Any time I travel to the city where they live, I always like to stop by at their home to visit with them. Usually, I meet only the children at home. The last time I visited, I met Mrs. Phillips at home. She was so delighted that she talked and talked and talked! It was surprising to me because I have always reckoned her to be a quiet woman. So I was wondering why she was talking so hard. I did not have to search very far for my answers. Jennifer, who is the eldest child of the Phillips family, is a good friend of mine. I asked, and she told me, what her parents' courtship was like. It was a very 'righteous' one. They didn't get to see each other regularly, they did not visit each other at home, no gifts, no shaking hands, no letters, nothing! It was as strict as it could get. Today, Mr. and Mrs. Phillips cannot communicate effectively, even after five children and several years of marriage! So Mrs. Phillips seizes any and every opportunity to discuss things with whoever cares to give an ear.

Why those rules and regulation during their courtship? They wanted to keep themselves pure till marriage. In keeping themselves pure, they laid the foundation poorly. They neglected the essentials of a courtship.

So how can we avoid the extremes without falling prey to the double diamond of death? How can we avoid the extremes? To the right and to the left, how far is too far? These and many more questions are asked every day. It is my aim with this book to prevent young men and women in relationships from falling prey to heartbreak, regret, shame, guilt, and disappointment that go with sex during courtship. It's also my aim to prevent these young people from embracing the path of deadly "over-carefulness." These two extremes are terrible materials for setting up a marriage. I call them the double diamond of death!

"And ye shall know the truth, and the truth shall make you free."[a]

Wow! I'm in Love!

Hold it. Don't celebrate yet! Are you sure you are in love, really in love? I'm sure you feel butterflies in your tummy. No doubt, any time you see her, your head does a 360-degree spin. Obviously, he makes your heart skip a beat. I do not doubt the fact that there are actions. My question is this: Are you sure those actions actually translate to love?

We have so humiliated love that, if it were possible, it would disappear from this generation. We have a "thousand and five" love clichés. We have developed theories on love. Any feeling that makes the penis of a man become erect is called love! "Love doesn't cost a thing." "Love is blind." "Love is wicked." These are clichés that have been hurled unjustly at love. For God's sake, when did love become wicked? Correct me if I'm wrong, but that would pass for the greatest irony of all time! So what, then, is love?

Check the dictionary, and you'll be more confused than you currently are. You'll be so confused that your name could change to Confucius. Ironically, the man that bore that name was not so confused. Let's look at some dictionary definitions.

1. "To feel tender affections for somebody." I guess having a soft spot for somebody could be synonymous with this definition. We have such feelings especially with members of our family. But they are not limited to people! We can also have the same affection for an ideal, a place, and even an animal!

2. "To feel desire for somebody." This desire is usually sexual, or should we say selfish?

3. "To like something very much." Did you say, "I love oranges"?

4. "To show kindness to somebody." Sometimes this kindness does not flow from within but from a sense of duty. I guess you know you are supposed to love your enemy?

5. "To have sex with somebody." Some people actually call it "making love"! The sound of that is really scary. It gives me the feeling that sex is a manufacturing company where love is made and probably placed on the shelf for sale!

Going through the dictionary, we can find about fifteen different meanings of love. Of course, these meanings come from the use of the word. That sort of compounds the problem. So two people can say, "I love you" to each other and mean totally different things! Consider this small example. The words in parentheses would represent the motive/meaning of the statement. John says to Linda, "I love you. (I want to have sex with you)." Linda smiles and says, "That's really touching. I love you too. (I love you just as I love my cat.)" Funny thing is that there is no way to find out what is truly meant. Or maybe there is a way. Well, let's not jump the gun. Right now, we are trying to find out what love truly is.

We could not get help from the dictionary, so let's turn to literature. And who else should we turn to other than the most acclaimed writer of all time? William Shakespeare. If we are going to take a look at William's work, none deserves our attention more than his most acclaimed work: Romeo and Juliet!

Shakespeare's Romeo and Juliet has been acclaimed as the greatest love story ever told. It is the story of two young lovers whose desire to be together against the wishes of their feuding families ultimately makes them take their own lives, as they are not prepared to endure life without each other. This is probably the most moving love story ever told. It has drawn tears from both young and old and will continue to draw tears. A lot of people have taken and idealized this story; they have made it their secret love expectation. Every lady imagines she is Juliet and hopes to find her Romeo! It is all very touching and sentimental until …

Oh my God! The whole story unfolds in a whooping … four days. Four days!

They get married the day after they meet and are, two days later, ready to kill themselves for somebody who did not exist five days earlier!

Wait a minute. There seems to be something else! How old was Juliet? She was really old, I guess. She was thirteen years old! Did she even understand what she was doing? It seems like our dearly beloved Romeo, who was also immature and naïve, secretly deceived and married this innocent, naïve girl in the name of love!

Wow! And we thought we had found the meaning of love. This was nothing but child abuse!

What, then, is love?

Drugged by Love?

I'll tell you a story.

It was the beginning of a new semester; it was not just any semester, but the semester! It was the first semester of John's final year. It looked like he started his final year on a poor note—he was late to his first class! Maybe that was just fate. He entered the class and scanned the faces for a friendly one, and then he locked eyes with Mabel. She had such a sweet smile. Thank the skies, there was a free seat besides her. They instantly became friends, and in a few days, they started a relationship. About a year later, they were married! Is that love? Yeah, people call that love at first sight!

You are a guy, and a beautiful girl walks into the room. In a nanosecond, you size up the situation: simple but modest clothing, a kind voice, and a million-dollar smile. Yep. She's definitely a woman, and you are attracted.[b]

You are a girl, and a handsome guy walks into the room. Your brain tells you that he's good looking, but you tell yourself to be careful because he may also be a jerk. So you watch carefully as he treats everyone with respect, and then he begins paying attention to you. Oh, no. Now what are you going to do? You are attracted to this guy.

The above scenarios have been playing out for a long time, and you know what? They will continue to play out. The problem, though, is that many people have titled it "love."

Oddly, it seems what we, people, have been calling love is not love at all. Before we talk about what love is, let's look at what people have unwarily mistaken for love.

It is called infatuation! Some modest people like to simply call it physical attraction, but I tell you the truth: it is more than mere attraction. The feelings and dynamics of love are there, but people tend to throw in the towel when things stop going the way they want. I'm sure you know what infatuation is. You have heard about it many times, but we are going to look at it from a very practical angle. Much of what we call love is actually infatuation! It is usually wise to understand what love and infatuation are, because it is difficult to be truthful to one's self when under the hold of these powerful forces! It is widely said that love is blind; in the actual sense, it is infatuation that is!

From the beginning of the world, the need for companionship has plagued man. The desire to love and to be loved in return is something we cannot wish away; in fact, it is a perfectly "legal" desire. It is harped and amplified by the "million and five" love songs that pervade the airwaves. It is in the movies; it is everywhere. The hero saves a beautiful girl from a terrible drug lord, falls in love with her, and they live happily ever after. We have come to believe that love is something we fall in! This is especially scary because it gives me the impression that love is a well or a pit that one can carelessly and accidentally fall into. I guess I'd better watch my steps. Truth is we are not only deceived by the music and the movies, but our brains also deceive us!

An article titled "Infatuation or Love?" claims that passionate or romantic love is like a drug in the human brain.

That's exactly what a team of scientists is discovering as they watch new love literally blaze its trail across the living brain. Using real-time MRI brain images of people in the initial throes of passion, they're finding that love originates far from the brain's logic center. In fact, love may vie for the same real estate in the brain as drug addiction. "There's this general craving-and-desire system that's engaged, only in this case the desire isn't for money or a drug or power or freedom. The desire is for merging with another person," explained co-researcher Arthur Aron, a professor of psychology at the State University of New York at Stony Brook.[b]

Explaining what actually goes on in our brains when we are attracted to somebody, a National Geographic article titled "Love: The Chemical Reaction," said, "In the right proportions, dopamine creates intense energy, exhilaration, focused attention and motivation to win rewards." Scientists have discovered that at the same time, we develop a serotonin imbalance similar to people who have obsessive-compulsive disorder. The article goes on to say, "Love and mental illness may be difficult to tell apart."[c]

Like most of us, what these scientists are calling love is in actual sense infatuation. That is why almost any time we hear about love, it is painted as something we fall into. It is painted as an accidental event or occurrence. You meet the guy, and after a few minutes, you fall in love. You say that because you feel butterflies in your tummy and your heart beats faster. It is actually not your tummy or your heart that is acting out, it is you brain! Your hormones are at war! Because it is your hormones, you cannot make life-based decisions on them! Remember what happens when you are in danger? Adrenalin kicks into action: it makes you either want to fight or take flight. At such times, you can practically do the impossible. You can even scale a high fence! Will you, because you scaled a high fence when a crazed buffalo was chasing you, suddenly decide to compete in the Olympics as a high jumper? That would be disastrous, to say the least. The bitter truth is that many of us make that type of decision when it comes to love. We claim to be high jumpers—or should we say lovers?—because adrenalin—or should we say dopamine?—was secreted!

I will illustrate this with another true-life story.

Pastor Johnson was a very anointed man of God with special grace for discipleship. He had many young people swarming around him, seeking his counsel for direction in life. He had a sublime way of reaching out to his followers. Emma was one of them. She was tall and beautiful, smart and witty. She had come to him about a young man she was interested in. They had been friends for long and were planning to take their relationship to another level. Pastor Johnson gave all the necessary counsel and prayed for them.

After about one year of a very successful and exemplary courtship, Peter, Emma's fiancé, reported to Pastor Johnson that she had run off with some other guy. This was really strange to the pastor, because Emma never made such important decisions without informing him.

Emma refused to speak with the pastor or with anybody that would give her good counsel. All she wanted was to be left alone. Like all things done improperly, her newfound love did not last. In no time, she was at the pastor's office in tears. According to her, she had had a crush on Sam when she was in high school, and seeing him after so many years brought all the old feelings back. Without thinking, she dropped God, her fiancé, her life coach, and every valuable thing, to run off with some guy she thought she was in love with.

According to Emma, "I was having feelings for Sam that I have not had for my fiancé."

So was she really in love with Sam?

The simple line of divide between love and infatuation is feelings! Infatuation feels good when affections are returned and feels bad when affections are spurned! That is all there is to it: feelings!

So for the umpteenth time, what is love?

Feelings + Time = Love?

The direction of infatuation is inward; the direction of love is outward! Infatuation is selfish; love is giving! The Bible tells us that "God so *loved* the world that He *gave* ..."[d] (emphasis mine)! That is what love does—it gives. Although it has been said that love is something we fall into, the truth is love is something we grow into; love is something we do!

In Greek, the language of the New Testament, there are three words for "love." One is *eros*, which refers to a romantic or sexual love. Another is *philia*, which means brotherly love or friendship. And the third is *agape*, a broader word used to describe God's outflowing love.[e] A good marriage will have all three kinds of love. Romance and romantic feelings are good and should be a part of a healthy marriage, but a relationship should not be based just on romantic feelings. Friendship and companionship with good communication are also part of a healthy marriage.

True love goes beyond friendship. True love will have and demonstrate outflowing, caring love. This is the type of love that God expresses toward mankind. It is the kind of love that is listed as part of the fruit of the Spirit.[f]

This kind of love takes time to develop. It goes beyond feelings and emotions. This real love or outgoing concern means being willing to set our own desires aside in order to provide for the needs of the other, and to give of ourselves even when the dopamine and serotonin have settled down and we are back to reality.

Again, it takes time for real love to grow. It doesn't happen at first sight. It doesn't happen only if or when we find a soul mate, and it is not something we fall into.

> Notice what the apostle Paul says about true love:
> Love never gives up. Love cares more for others than for self. Love doesn't want what it doesn't have. Love doesn't strut, doesn't have a swelled head, doesn't force itself on others, isn't always "me first," doesn't fly off the handle, doesn't keep score of the sins of others, doesn't revel when others grovel, takes pleasure in the flowering of truth, puts up with anything, trusts God always, always looks for the best, never looks back, but keeps going to the end.[g]

This is outgoing love. Notice that this love does not seek its own. This means not focusing on self or on what you can get out of a relationship but on what you have to give and contribute to a relationship.

Natural attraction for the opposite sex is something that praying and fasting will not take away. It will always be there. But when not handled properly, these simple and harmless affections can quickly become lust, infatuation! The problem with infatuation is that there are no boundaries. The individual is at this time under the spell of his raging hormones. It takes wisdom and a lot of determination to tame such feelings. But with love, there is something else. It is called boundaries. It is these boundaries that create room for well-informed decisions. Under the spell of infatuation, anything that pleases you goes. It is difficult to stop a raging bush fire in the midst of very dry grasses. Even with true love, even with all the boundaries, a lot of things that are not bargained for still happen, talk less of emotions running wild and free in the name of love.

It is important to be sure that you have not been taken over by the deceitful appeal of infatuation. If you have, close this book and first of all get rid of that feeling. It is the issues that arise inside the walled boundaries of love I am concerned about, not emotions that have run amok!

I received mail some time ago from a friend. It was a test to help check if what a person presently calls love is actually infatuation. I'll reproduce that mail for you here. I believe it's going to be of immense help.

The Twelve Tests of Love[h]

Each of the following tests is designed to help you **discern and distinguish between love and infatuation**. After you read each statement, apply it to your current relationship, or to your expectations of what a love-relationship should include. Ask yourself: Is my current relationship or my view of relationships more in alignment with love or infatuation in this particular area? Write an "L" for love and an "I" for infatuation alongside each of the tests. If your relationship is over 51 percent love by the standard of the test, write an "L" in the margin; if it's 51 percent or more on the infatuation side, put an "I." This isn't a test that you can fail. It's a tool to help you grow in your understanding of loving another human being.

__**1. The Test of Time.** *Love benefits and grows through time; infatuation ebbs and diminishes with time.*

__**2. The Test of Knowledge.** *Love grows out of an appraisal of all the known characteristics of the other person.*

__**3. The Test of Focus.** *Genuine love is other-person centred. Infatuation is self-centred.*

__**4. The Test of Singularity.** *Genuine love is focused on only one person. An infatuated individual may be "in love" with two or more persons simultaneously.*

__**5. The Test of Security.** *Genuine love requires and fosters a sense of security and feelings of trust.*

__**6. The Test of Work.** *An individual in love works for the other person, for his or her mutual benefit.*

__**7. The Test of Problem Solving.** *A couple in love faces problems frankly and tries to solve them. Infatuated people tend to disregard or try to ignore problems.*

__**8. The Test of Distance.** *Love knows the importance of distance. Infatuation imagines love to be intense closeness, 24/7, all the time.*

__**9. The Test of Physical Attraction.** *Physical attraction is a relatively small part of genuine love, but it is the center focus of infatuation.*

__**10. The Test of Affection.** *In love, affection is expressed later in the relationship, involving the external expression of the physical attraction we just described.*

__**11. The Test of Stability.** *Love tends to endure. Infatuation may change suddenly and unpredictably.*

__**12. The Test of Delayed Gratification.** *A couple in genuine love is not indifferent to the timing of their wedding, but they do not feel an irresistible drive toward it. An infatuated couple* tends to feel an urge to get married—instantly. Postponement for the infatuated is intolerable.

I hope taking this text was a process that has helped you see more clearly the differences between love and infatuation. As tempting as it may be to jump into relationships without forethought, stop long enough to ask whether you really want the results that the Hollywood formula delivers or whether you want to pursue the adventure of doing love God's way.

Story Time

Milk in the Beautiful Cup![i]

General Sisera was running for his life. He never imagined that he'd ever be at this point. He could never have imagined that he, the most feared soldier in the territory, would turn his back on the battleground. But he did. He was on the run—literally! Now he was thirsty as hell! *All I need to do, he thought, is to safely reach the house of Heber. We've been friends for long; I know I can get plenty of water. And there is Jael, his lovely wife to keep me company.* So he hurried on, stealing a look or two over his shoulder. He was beginning to feel someone was following. Apart from that, there was something else—the cries of his fellow soldiers!

The cries of his fellow soldiers being slaughtered were too much for him to bear. He had trained them to be fearless. He had always told them that the first rule of combat was "never turn your back on your enemies." He had habitually ordered the death of soldiers who had become too scared to continue the fight. Worse still, he usually brought them to an open square and let prostitutes, the lowest cadre of women, kill them. That was the most embarrassing death a soldier could possibly have. He had taught them that any man killed by a woman was worse than a dog. Today, however, he had broken his own laws. He was on the run. But who could blame him? After all, the battle had been going so well, until hail started to fall from the sky. The amazing thing though was that the hail only fell on his soldiers. He could not explain how something like that could have happened. Something like a boulder had fallen on his left shoulder. He could not imagine what it was. He was sure it was not hail. How could hail be that big?

He had performed the usual rituals before marching his men out. The priests had demanded the heads of five firstborn sons. They had stolen secretly through the night to kidnap the boys. He personally watched the priest slaughter and offer them to Molech, their god. So what could have gone wrong? It looked like the whole world, including the stars, were fighting him!

An arrow tore past him, narrowly missing his ears. That jolted him from his thoughts and back to reality. He doubled his steps and started to run in a zigzag to avoid the arrows that were now pouring in. He knew if he was going to be safe at Heber's house, he was going to have to lose his pursuers. He deftly maneuvered his way through the undulating slopes and hills that marked the area. He thought about his iron chariots, which would have made his escape easier.

He wondered what would have happened to the nine hundred iron chariots and their horses he had spent years building and training. He had jumped off his chariot when he heard a strange and fearful shout from behind him. He thought they had been ambushed! There was no time to investigate. So he had leapt off his chariot and twisted through the many caves and caverns that decorated Mount Tabor. Now he had to do something quick before his pursuers caught up with him.

He ran into a circular cave. Such caves abounded in the area. Circular caves led from the entrance into several openings but back to the entrance. At the time he was out of the cave, his pursuers were at a safe distance ahead. He turned and took a short route he knew so well. He had always stolen through this path at night, especially when he wanted to consort with one of his many prostitutes. This day, the road was leading somewhere else. It was leading to the house of a man whose wife had defiantly resisted his approaches. It did not matter now, but somehow he hoped Jael would welcome him with more than water.

He sped down the lonely road. His pursuers must have given up on him now. As he ran along, panting like a tired dog, he traced the road as it wired down the hilly horizon, away from the raving eyes of telltales.

The road wound through Scorpion's Pass. This pass was so named because it was rumored that scorpions the size of a man's head patrolled it. Sisera knew it was not true. He had taken that road several times. From Scorpion's Pass, it led through two caves and then through Blood Stream. It was so called because the water was red from the blood of soldiers and civilians killed by Sisera. Just beyond the stream, there were palm trees looking up to Heber's house.

Just a little while now, he would be running through the palm trees. Something told him his pursuers would still be on him. A battle was not won if the king or the commander of the enemy's army was still alive. Today, the price tag on his head was great.

Just beyond the palm trees, he saw Heber's house. What a relief. Soon, he would be safe.

He hurried along, stealing glances over his shoulder. In one last effort, he dashed into Heber's tent, knocking down a bowl or two as he tried to run into the inner room.

Now inside, he scanned the room. It looked deserted. He wondered where Heber was. Just then, he heard a sound behind a curtain. With the silence of a skilled assassin, he crept toward the curtain, and with a speed comparable to that of thunder, he yanked off the curtain and pointed his sword at whoever was there.

The scream that emanated was that of a woman. It was Jael! Quickly apologizing, he asked for a bowl of water. He was extremely tired and panting from the long race. He was bruised and badly injured.

Lying on a well-prepared bed, Sisera was thanking his stars. Today could turn out to be the day he had been waiting for. Jael was acting especially nice today. She had promised to treat his wounded shoulder.

She had led him to a floor bed that was especially soft. What could she possibly have in mind? Maybe she had given in to him at last, or maybe the sight of an injured man aroused her! As if fate had planned it all along, Heber was not home! He congratulated himself. He had forgotten about the war. He only knew now that he needed water. He called out to Jael for more water.

In a moment, she was back. He wondered what had taken her so long. He stopped wondering the moment he saw her. She was coming with a beautifully crafted, Persian, gold cup that was used only by kings. Only a few wealthy people had such cups. He felt proudly important. Jael serving him water in that cup only meant one thing—she had fallen for him.

He wanted to take the cup, but Jael refused to release it. She eased him back into the bed and held the cup to his mouth. He closed his eyes as his lips touched the cup. He felt on top of the world. He was royalty again. As the liquid poured into his mouth, he tasted something different from water. It was thick and sweet, sweeter than water. He somehow knew it would not quench his thirst, but he felt there was no need to spoil the fun of the moment. He slurped as the milk found its way down his throat. He licked his lips and told Jael to go outside to check for pursuers. She was to tell he was not there.

By the time she returned, he was already drifting off. Jael waited a few minutes for the concentrated milk to take full effect. In a matter of seconds, he was already deeply asleep. She looked at him, feeling nothing but hate for the man that had been a constant thorn in her flesh. He had prodded her both night and day. Most annoying was the fact that he was her husband's friend. Today, however, she hated him for another reason, a reason totally strange to her. It was as though a hateful spirit had taken her over. She saw how weak and defenseless he looked. Remembering the voices of people begging for mercy as he killed them at Blood Stream, she grabbed a tent pin that was lying on the floor. It had been knocked down when he came hurriedly inside. She scanned the room for something, and found it sitting on a table at the edge of the room.

Armed with the hammer and tent pin, she knelt beside his head, unstrapped his helmet, and stroked his hair. He was muttering something from his sleep. She did not care what he was saying. She only knew a new Blood Stream would soon be discovered in her room. She tied his hands behind him.

Gripping the hammer firmly at the wooden handle, she set the tent pin on his temple. With one powerful swing, she hit the tent pin, driving it through his head and into the ground.

The struggle did not last for so long. Jael sat on his legs, holding him firmly to the ground. After a few minutes of struggling violently, he slowed down.

Meanwhile, Sisera had been dreaming. He was dreaming of a river of milk. He swam around with Jael by his side. All of a sudden, she was gone, the milk became red like crimson, and it became Blood Stream. He started to swim violently out of the water, but somehow he could not move. His legs were stuck. In one last gasp, he struggled. But he had lost his strength; he was sinking in the crimson tide. Then everything went black.

Jael knew he was dead. She covered him with a cloth. She left the room and waited outside for the uninvited guest she was certain was going to come.

In a few minutes, she heard the sound of a chariot running into view. There was no mistake: it was the chariot of Barak, the commander of Israel's army. He was also on the chase of Sisera. Jael wasted no time. She came out into full view and called to Barak.

Now inside, Barak saw his adversary dead in a woman's room, killed by a woman. Somehow, he felt embarrassed that the victory of the day had gone to a woman, but he also felt pleased that the fiery Sisera died in the hands of a woman. That was the worst death a soldier could get.

The battle was over, the war was won, and the victory was sealed. This battle though was won in a tent. It was fought between a warrior and a housewife. It was won with a beautiful cup and concentrated milk! The woman came out unscathed; the warrior was in a bloody stream!

Motives and actions are never always the same.

Appearances do not always align with *inpearances.*

Containers do not normally describe contents.

Outwards do not always tell the truth about inwards.

Sweet taste does not always mean okay.

Like Sisera …

✦ We see the beautiful cup and our pride blinds our eyes!

✦ We taste the milk and our desires shut down our reason!

✦ We see a woman (man) and our caution drops dead!

✦ We give her (him) the nail and the hammer and say, "Dear, play on my head while I'm asleep!"

Bonds: Electrovalent or Covalent!

Cynthia, a beautiful and elegant lady who had modesty as second nature, was struggling with memories of a past that threatened to extinguish the light of her future. She had successfully hidden these battles from the view of everyone, including her parents. Her secrets have remained with her; she was prepared to take them with her to the grave. There was one thing that had always troubled her though; it was the thought of how she was going to reveal these things to her husband. She wondered if she would have to tell him before or after the wedding. The thought of what his reaction was going to be was very unsettling for her. She had almost made up her mind to stay single! There was something else—she felt worthless!

Joshua was a young pastor. He had a peculiar grace for counseling young people. He had received a series of young people with open arms. His counsel had given them a new inspiration for life. He worshipped in the same church with Cynthia. In fact, they were friends. He invited her over to his house because he had a few things to discuss with her. He actually sensed she was deeply troubled in the spirit.

She couldn't hide it anymore. She broke down in tears as she told him her heartrending story. Joshua shook within. He tried to control the tremors that were now growing in his body. He wondered how possible it was for a lady with Cynthia's modesty to have lived the kind of life she had just described. Little wonder she felt her life was over.

He swung into action, describing to her the principles of leaving the past in the past and how much her future was more important than her past. He made her understand that it was gross injustice to chain herself to the past. He drew up a counseling schedule; they had a regular meeting place where they were to discuss. He was going to take her through a process of self-reevaluation. They were going to pray together, he was going to give her a few assignments, and he was sure she was going to be all right. After all, he had used the same methods for several people.

The counseling sessions started. She never missed a day. Everything went according to plan. She was beginning to have a high sense of self-esteem. She was no longer scared of the past. She concluded that the blood of Jesus was enough to wipe her clean. She came to see herself as fresh as new. But that was not all. She was also in love!

She had *fallen* in love with Joshua. She imagined that such a man that could tolerate her past with such grace must be an angel. Even though the counseling sessions were over, she still found herself wanting to see Joshua. Joshua was also having strange feelings for her. He wondered what it was but could not fathom it. Cynthia desired more and more of Joshua's attention. Everything that happened to her was a story she eagerly wanted to tell Joshua. Joshua started to unconsciously treat her specially. Soon though, he realized that what he felt was more of compassion than love. His compassion had made him throw caution to the wind. Unfortunately, she was already hooked. He knew he could not free himself from her without breaking her heart. What had he done wrong? Was there something he could have done better?

It is true that many people mistake infatuation for love, it is also true that many times people put themselves in impossible situations! There is a growth pattern and process of love. Anything other than this normal process is a journey into a lion's den.

When two people are in constant contact, they become fond of each other. Do you remember your first day at nursery school? You were so lonely; there was no familiar face. Suddenly out of nowhere, somebody comes around and begins to chat with you. You talk for a while and walk around. Almost in an instant, you bond. The next day, you introduce that person as your *best friend!* How did that person suddenly become your best friend? More appropriately, that person should have been introduced as your *only friend*! Truth is that is what happens when two people are in constant isolated contact. By isolated, I mean no intrusion. He is your only friend. There is no other person competing for your attention. When two males or two females are in constant isolated contact, they become close, very close. They'd like to describe themselves as "best friends." If that can happen between friends of the same sex, then imagine the possibilities …

By default, we are wired to get attracted to the opposite sex. Research has shown that a large proportion of daughters are closer to their dads, just as the reverse is the case with sons. The sons were said to be closer to their mothers. It is not just because of unequal attention, it is because males have been wired to be attracted to females just as the females are wired to be attracted to males. So imagine a constant isolated contact between a male and a female. The attraction that will develop would be a bombshell. Here, we would not be talking of best friends; we would be talking of … bonded mates!

Bonding is basically the linking between people in a relationship. But the kind of bond that is formed in this kind of relationship we are describing is more than a link; it is fiery!

When you compare the feelings and emotions that are generated in this kind of relationship, you'll find that they match with those of a relationship based on *true love*. So you cannot simply take the twelve tests of love to validate your feelings! This kind of friendship leads invariably to the same destination as infatuation, but it is difficult to detect—except you agree to look closely. You'll find yourself making the same decisions and choices you'd make if it were really true love. In fact, such choices are made with relative ease. At surface level, the feelings and emotions in this friendship would fit perfectly to the description of love in 1 Corinthians 13! I'm sure the burning question now is this: how do we differentiate? We will come to that in a few minutes! But first, let's talk chemistry. I'm sure some of you will find the ideas strange, so I'm going to try to be as elementary as possible.

In inorganic chemistry, we are told that we have several chemical elements making up our planet and the universe at large. Usually, a large proportion of these elements are unstable because of their formation. No element is satisfied in that unstable state, so they are constantly looking for ways to stabilize. As a result, a lot of chemical reactions take place. These reactions take place by the formation of bonds between two or more of these elements. Usually, these bonds give the elements certain level of stability. The newly bonded elements become new elements, or compounds as chemistry would call them.

A common example is water. Water, with the formula H_2O, is formed when hydrogen (H) and oxygen (O) form a bond. Two hydrogen atoms come together to form a bond with one oxygen atom. So we have two male hydrogen atoms getting married to one oxygen atom forming a *couple* called water. That sounds like polyandry right? In the world of chemical elements, things do not exactly work that way. So bonding is a part of life for chemical elements. But that's not the entire story—there is something else! There are different kinds of bonding! For the sake of keeping it simple, we will look only at two of the easiest and simplest kinds. We have the electrovalent and the covalent bonds.

To explain these bonds, I'll use the table salt. You know the importance of salt to your food, don't you? I'll bet you'll pour your food away if there's no salt. The chemical name for table salt is sodium chloride; the chemical formula is NaCl. It is formed from bonding between sodium and chlorine. This is going to be a little technical.

All chemical elements have some things that look like orbits. These orbits contain things that look like little planets called electrons. Each orbit can contain a maximum of eight electrons. When the outer orbit has fewer than eight, the element becomes unstable. It begins to look for a way to get a complete orbit.

Sodium, like all other elements, has orbits and electrons. The problem with sodium, however, is that it has only one electron on its outer orbit. On the other hand, chlorine has seven. So while chlorine needs one electron, sodium needs seven, or better still needs to lose one. Usually, sodium would agree to lose its lone electron to chlorine that is desperately in need of one. Now we have sodium that is rid of one electron, and chlorine that has gained one electron. This kind of bond is called electrovalent bond. On the alternative, sodium can decide to retain its lone electron but agree to share it with chlorine. So chlorine with its seven electrons signs a joint ownership agreement with sodium. Technically, the one electron of sodium belongs to chlorine as well as its seven electrons belong to sodium. This kind of bond is called a covalent bond. (Technically, sodium does not form a covalent bond with chlorine. I used this example to keep things simple enough.) In the two instances, a bond is formed; the difference is in the *how*.

The electrovalent bond has all the features of a sincere and kind relationship. Its motives look very sincere, but on a closer look, we find the truth. Let us examine this bond.

Electrovalent Bond *Mates*

There are arguments that this is a very sincere bond with noble intentions. No doubt, the intentions look good, but are they really good? Let's look at a few of those arguments.

1. Sodium had only one electron, and he gave it out. Does that not resemble God's love in giving his only begotten son? That is a very good point. Define selflessness! He had only one, but he gave it. The question is *why?* On the surface, this act of giving is selfless and flawless, but when probed with a microscope, we discover that the true motive behind this giving is not that of care but that of a selfish ambition. Sodium gave it away because he wanted to become stable, period. In many relationships, especially those that are formed from constant isolated contacts, a lot of good deeds are done. On the surface, they look innocent and faultless, but there is always an underlying selfish reason for the action. Usually, all actions are toward sustaining a satisfaction of having all the attention of the other. Joshua, in the opening story, gave all his time and attention to Cynthia. He was secretly enjoying the attention and the inner satisfaction of achievement. Cynthia was at the receiving end, and she read his action as loving care! But the truth is that though his action seemed selfless, it was meeting a selfish need.

2. Chlorine could have given that space to any other electron, but she decided to give it to this homeless sodium electron. She already had her bag full and had only one available space to share. If she had been in Bethlehem, she would have made room for pregnant Mary. But let us not forget that she had a purpose in mind, a selfish purpose. But apart from the jostle for stability, there is also the motive of colonization.

Chlorine cannot imagine sharing her "electron" with anyone. She needs him by her side all the time. She wants to wake up and see him there all the time. If anybody dares to come close, she will make sure she keeps him out. Electrovalent bonds have been said to be very strong. That in reality is very true. A selfish force makes one party to shield the other from having any form of relationship with others. Apart from being selfish, it is also fearful. The fear of competition, the fear of losing him to somebody else. But the Bible in no uncertain terms says, "Perfect love drives out fear![a]"

3. Hydrogen is devoted. He focuses all his attention on chlorine. He has no time to be looking out at strange women. His favorite Scripture is Job 31:1. Like Job, he made a covenant with his eyes not to look lustfully upon a maid. But tell me what kind of love destroys relationships with others. How can you claim to have love when you have abandoned other people that genuinely care about you? That is not love; it is madness! True and sincere love cares about other people. How can chlorine trust hydrogen's love when it was so easy for him to leave and totally forget the ones that used to be very close to him? Is it out of sight, out of mind? If hydrogen could so easily forget the others he used to care about, what makes chlorine think he would not soon forget her? She knows this, which is why she refuses to let go.

4. Electrovalent bonds require great force to break apart. The binding force is very strong. This should be a praiseworthy thing, but it is not! Every true and sincere relationship is founded on trust. As the trust grows, the relationship solidifies. The source of strength in true love-based relationships is trust. But in this kind of electrovalent

relationship, the source of strength is fear, a lack of trust. Chlorine is not sure sodium would stay. So the fear makes her do a lot of desperate things to make sure he cannot look elsewhere. On the surface, it would look as though she was putting effort to make things work! This effort is driven by a fear that stems from a lack of trust!

5. Hydrogen and chlorine boast of an unwavering commitment to each other. The close-ended nature of the bond makes it impossible to commit elsewhere. Because electrovalent relationships are close ended, there is a rapid growth of mutual affection. This makes both parties want to spend more time together. As a result, they begin to pay less attention to other necessities—people, work, activities, etc. But most scary of all, they begin to pay less attention to God. Their heavenward activities begin to dwindle. They are just satisfied with themselves. This leads to something they never bargained for: a strange desire to know more, to keep wanting more. This is usually the stage where the damage gets done; it is also the stage where the eyes get opened. At this time, there is a height of uncontrollable passion. Both parties get physically involved. Sometimes, one party may get aggressive!

Let me share a very true but painful story with you.

He was a banker with prospects. There was always something about him; everybody who met him knew he was not just passing by. He had a focus in life. Above all, he was a very strong born-again Christian. We shall call him Kunle.

She was a banker with uncommon grace. Everybody wondered what kind of lady she was; she could do things even men could not do. Exceptional! That's what could best describe her. To ice the cake, she was a very devout Christian. We shall call her Anne.

Kunle and Anne met in the bank and became friends. Their friendship was ordained by God; a lot of wonderful things were happening through them. As a team, their impact was felt in the bank. Together, they developed killer ideas that improved the fortunes of the bank. The boss was full of praise for the duo. They were virtually the talk of the bank. Everyone said they were made in heaven. As Christians, their impact was also hell threatening! They caused a revival in the bank. Any time they had an opportunity to address their fellow bankers, they did it with so much zeal and passion, spitting fire from their lips. Both physically and spiritually, they were making an impact.

As friends, they were not doing badly. They studied and prayed together, watched each other's back, and made sure they both stayed focused and on track.

Everyone believed they were made from heaven. They were just too perfect to be earthlings! Their colleagues felt they were too good to be friends. Everyone wanted them to get married. It was not only the other bankers that felt so; Kunle and Anne felt the same way. But there was a little problem.

Kunle was already engaged to somebody else!

Let's back up a little.

Kunle, a born-again Christian serving the Lord with all his heart, though engaged, is in love with Anne!

Anne, a fire-branded lady only comparable to the biblical Deborah, is in love with Kunle!

Ordinarily, anybody can be in love with anyone. Given the right circumstances, love can develop. So let's not be too quick in crucifying them.

Kunle's friendship with Anne almost ruined his relationship with his fiancée. He spoke less and less with her; all his attention was on Anne. And so gradually they drifted. Kunle felt things he really did not feel for his fiancée. Not all the boundaries seemed to matter anymore. He had become addicted—addicted to Anne!

One day, Kunle paid Anne a visit. They talked and played for some time. And then … lip action!

And then … heavy petting!

And then … God came just in time!

Did you ask what happened?

I don't know!

Now it's my turn to ask. "What happened to Kunle and Anne? How did they get to lose it? What were they thinking?"

They knew what was right; they'd preached it, counseled young people about it, and lived it all their lives! How come they just dropped everything?

The truth is they allowed themselves to get to a stage where they had lost control. They developed an electrovalent bond!

Let us return to our discussion, shall we?

If this were a court, it would be unfair to electrovalent bonds not to hear covalent bonds give their defense. So we'd try to poke our hands in covalent bond's eyes and see how he would fare.

Covalent Bond *Mates*

We saw how the true actions of the guys who were electrovalently bonded were backed by petty selfishness. How about covalent bonds? Are they also playing the same game?

1. Hydrogen had only one electron, but he decided to share. That seems to say he is not selfish. But wait a minute; is it not true that his real purpose for sharing was to gain stability status? Yeah, that is so true. But there is a slight difference. This is not a proud I-can-boast-about-it style. He needed stability, and he went after it in the best possible way. Don't we all find love to get rid of that instability that is caused by loneliness?

2. Chlorine seems to be foolish. She is contributing seven electrons to the bond while hydrogen is contributing just one, yet they both enjoy the same stability! That is kind of true. But guess what? They are not complaining! Is that not what real love does—allow a couple to complement one another? Nobody cares who is contributing more; nobody cares who is more mature. There is joy in the fact that they are both achieving their aim.

3. Can you imagine the pain of bonding? Sodium and chlorine are entirely different. Sodium is classified as a metal while chlorine is a halogen (never mind the chemistry jargon). These are two different guys. They could have just taken the easy route, but they chose to stick it out together. It must have taken quite a lot of effort for a metal to have successfully joined with a halogen that is basically liquid. They patiently allowed time to contribute to their bonding!

4. Relationship! Even though he is bonded with chlorine, the lone sodium electron can still relate effectively and freely

with his own brother electrons. He also has the chance to become friends with other chlorine electrons. Freedom of association is a very crucial factor that douses the emotional effect of wanting too much from a mate. It gives both parties opportunity to grow both independently and together. Although their lives are intertwined, they do not live a life of absolute dependence on each other. It is also a sign of trust.

5. Trust! Sodium and chlorine have mutual trust for each other so they are not afraid of letting each other relate freely with others. This trust strengthens their love as their love grows; all forms of fear disappear. Their relationship gets stronger and stronger. It solidifies to the point where nothing can come between them. It is true that freedom to relate brings temptations. It is also true that they both have their weaknesses, but as long as their bond holds, they remain connected. This connection gives room for constant interaction. They bear each other's burden until the load becomes lighter. They, out of love and not fear, give caution and watch each other's back. In the final analysis, allowing themselves to go through fire strengthens them and makes them more prepared to face the challenges that come with life.

Every relationship ends up forming a bond, but the way the relationship is formed determines the kind of bond that is formed. The kind of bond that is formed would determine for the most part, the actions that the *lovers* would find themselves taking. An electrovalent bond relationship is covertly forceful. It develops rapidly and is cunningly selfish. A covalent bond relationship exemplifies love in its entirety, gives room for mistakes, and provides the mechanisms for correcting them.

How do you escape from falling into electrovalent bonds?

For starters, there is no need to get too close to anybody of the opposite sex. A lot of things beyond human control happen between males and females! It is better to have a wide variety of friends, male and female both. It is not a decision if there is only one option. Right decisions are gotten from proper judgment. But how can you judge when you only have one option? Let's throw sentiments aside. Having a lot of close friends makes it easy for us to learn about relationships. Making a decision becomes possible because there are alternatives. You may claim you don't need alternatives; you may say the Lord will tell you what to do. But wait a minute and answer my question. What do you expect the Lord to do? Stamp your choice? What if the Lord tells you that person is not his will? How easy will it be for you to accept? The point again is this: there is no need to invest emotions unnecessarily. If love would develop, it should grow naturally from your equal interaction with all your friends. There is no need to set yourself up for a journey you may not be able to control.

So make a comparison. Your relationship: which type is it? What kind of bond have you formed? Electrovalent or covalent?

Story Time

A Sword Unsheathed![b]

Weeping, she looked down at her white gown. Just few minutes ago, it was sparkling white. Then it was stained with her blood! She had been stabbed by a sword! It was not the stab from the conventional sword. This blood was caused by another kind of sword. Now she will never be able to wear this garment again. She could wash it clean, but she lost the right to wear it; she lost her pride; she just lost her virginity!

What was she thinking? Had she lost her mind? Hoping it was a bad dream that would soon end, she pinched herself. Now she knew the deed had been done; it was never going away! To make matters worse, it was not worth it! She had just discovered that the experience was overrated! She was beginning to imagine what her brothers were going to do when she got home. They must already be looking for her now.

Her father, Jacob, was a man who had experienced both the good and bad of life. His experience had humbled him. But her brothers! They were a bunch of Goody Two-shoes who never cared about others. They were always right. They believed they should get anything they wanted. Hook and crook meant the same thing to them! Thoughts flew about in her mind, mind-boggling thoughts. *What are they going to do when they find out? How did I get myself into this mess?*

Her family had just arrived from Mesopotamia, where they lived with her great uncle, Laban. She was the only girl in a family made up of twelve brothers and five parents apart from her. The journey had been one of several perils. At one time, everybody had been scared because Uncle Esau was coming to meet them with four hundred men! At another time, it was Laban who came chasing them. Things got worse! One morning, Jacob announced to the whole family that he couldn't sleep at night. Rachael was already worrying herself with what could possibly have gone wrong with her husband. Her worry was short-lived. He told them that he had spent the night fighting with an angel. Nobody believed him until he tried to walk! After all the perils of the journey, they had finally come to settle in Schechem. This was the first time in her life she was living among people other than her family; it was her first time away from *home*. Although she had her immediate family around, she felt the air smelled different; she felt the air smelled of freedom!

Looking again at the stain on her dress, she began to replay the scenes that led to it. She had just finished her chores that morning. She had cleaned her father's tent and served his breakfast. She had retired to her room to continue the coat she was knitting when she heard voices. They were coming closer and louder. She rushed out of her tent to see what the fuss was all about. People, a lot of them, were running excitedly toward a destination she was not aware of. Without remembering to tell anyone, she rushed out with the crowd. They were going to the temple of Asherah! She followed them till they reached the place. She tried to struggle her way through the crowd. She pushed and shoved until she got to the front. It was then she saw what everybody was eagerly running to see: the worship session!

The worship session was just starting. She saw everybody kneeling down. Not knowing what to do, she knelt down as well. She could trace the tiny figure of a man walking out of the temple and toward the crowd. He stopped when he got to the entrance and climbed a raised platform that looked like an altar with a flattened surface. Curiously, she looked on as the man jumped around while chanting songs she couldn't understand. Then all of a sudden, as if controlled by a spirit, he stopped and clapped his hands. A scantily clad woman came out and performed a strange dance on the platform. The next thing that followed shocked her to the bones! The man and the woman were having sex right on the platform!

She couldn't bear to watch, so she stood up, turned around, and ran out. Outside the temple area, she sat on a stone with a few other girls. They were discussing all sorts of lewd things. She had never seen or heard anything like this in all her life. How could people be so corrupt? She shifted uncomfortably, wanting to say something but not finding the courage to open her lips. That was when he came.

He was handsome and well built. He walked and talked as if he was royalty. He came to her and introduced himself as Schechem of Schechem! She had laughed heartily at the sound of that. He offered to teach her everything she wanted to know about the people. He was going to show her to the most beautiful ladies in the city; he was going to make her stay interesting. This was great. It was what she wanted. Finally, a friend! Never would she be alone. She loved her family and enjoyed their company, but now was a chance to be a grownup and to garner some experience for herself. So without hesitating, she had jumped at the idea. She immediately left the temple square with Schechem.

Everyone had been worried about her, because for the first time in her life she came home late. She promised not to let it happen again; she promised not to allow herself to get carried away. By the next day, she had totally forgotten about the promise.

It was the festival to Molech. Molech was a god foreign to the people, but since there was freedom of worship, every once in a while people loved to hang out and have fun, especially when the worship session involved actions other than endless chants.

So it continued, from one festival to another, from one place to the other. The both of them became an item in town. She heard some of the young men whispering about her, and she even had a few of them making passes at her. She thought very little of it.

"We are just friends." That was the answer she gave Jacob when he inquired about her closeness with Schechem. As far as she was concerned, there was no harm in being friends with him. Schechem had taken a top spot in her life; she had begun to enjoy his company and was having too much fun with him.

Her father asked her to remain indoors that day, but she had already promised Schechem she'd go out to see some friends with him. She sneaked out the house and ran off with Schechem and his friends. That was when he forced himself on her!

She was jerked back to reality with the sound of her name. *Surely,* she thought, *they've already started looking for me.* Her mind kept wandering; she kept asking herself, *How could he have done this to me? I thought he loved me.*

Schechem, still sitting on his bed, thought sorrowfully about what he had just done. How could he have forced himself on her? He loved her and did not ever have evil intentions. Or did he?

He had made her promise to go out to see some friends; he had insisted even when she told him of her father's instructions. He couldn't imagine spending a whole day without having her around. She had gotten to him deeply, touching him in all the soft places. *How did she get into my head this much?* he thought. *No lady has ever taken hold of me like this.*

Schechem, being the prince of his city, prided himself as being able to get any lady he wanted. They threw themselves at him, literally. At the prince's festival organized every year, ladies in their throngs competed vigorously to win the rights to spend a day with him. But for the first time, he felt insanely drawn to this stranger from Mesopotamia!

It had started very casually. He had only thought to show her around his city and school her in the ways of his people. But then, he had caught himself thinking about so many lewd things he could possibly do with her. He made light of it until the day he asked his men to beat up a young man he saw flirting with her.

His desire to have her alone to himself had grown so strong; it had grown to the point where he couldn't hold it back. Thinking back at how it had happened, he felt the splash of his tears on his foot.

They were together with friends in the house. It was a fun group; everyone was in high spirit except him. His mind had traveled to faraway places. The sounds of her laughter were like the sound of galloping horses taking them away to a secluded island. He could take no more of the mental torture; he had to get what he wanted. He had acted like a crazed goat, asking everyone to leave. He had gone on his knees asking Dinah to sleep with him, but she had refused. Like one possessed with a thousand demons, he had roared and grabbed her unto the bed, and with reckless abandon, he had unsheathed his *sword* and had repeatedly stabbed at her flower, despite her cries for help.

He shook his head vigorously, as if to shake off the memory of what had inevitably happened. His feet were all wet, as though they were dipped in a stream. In reality, they were.

The question he could not shake off his head was this: "How did this happen?"

The Day Wise King Solomon Got Confused

"**B**ehold, I have done according to your words. Lo, I have given you a wise and an understanding heart, so that there was none like you before you, and after you none shall arise like you."[a]

Have you ever been around somebody who seems to know everything? I have! I only caught them fumbling on rare occasions. Those occasions howbeit were very rare. Such people, we call them witty.

Let me tell you about one such person.

His name?

Jedidiah. Jedidiah Ben-David.

He was the son of a very powerful king. In fact, his father was the strongest king in the entire world, and his kingdom was dominating the earth. His father had fought so many victorious battles. He was so successful that other kingdoms had to bribe fellow kings to join them to war against him. He had killed all sorts of people and animals. He killed giants and minnows, lions and bears. He had the power of several men put together. He was in control of the strongest army the world could boast of. They were called the mighty men of David! He had men who would kill a lion inside a pit on a snowy day; men who would dispossess giants of their weapons; men who would single-handedly take on armies; men who would go into a garrison surrounded by deadly enemies to fetch a cup of water!

Wow! What a strong king. Guess what! None of these men could withstand him! What do you think? Jedidiah should be proud to have that kind of dad. None of his peers could boast of that. But all of a sudden, David, the king of the world, grows old and dies! Guess who the next king is supposed to be. That's right: Jedidiah! Nothing was stopping him from being king. After all, he was the king's son. It was just that the odds were against him. His father raised the bar too high. His father made such a name that to become a king was no longer a walk in the park! It was now a herculean task.

Unlike his father, Jedidiah was no warrior. He had never fought battles. He was raised in the peace and safety of the palace. Like his father, he was born late into the family, but unlike Dad, he was never in the bush tending sheep and killing lions and bears. He was in the backyard making castles in the sand! Dad had to pay a very steep bride price—one hundred foreskin of enemy soldiers,e not just any kind of enemy but terrifying ones! For him, it was a walk in the park. The ladies were practically falling head over heels in love with him. His dad had access to men of valor, soldiers of worth. He did not! His father's soldiers had grown old with him. Many of them had died. The mighty men of David had either become old men of David or dead men of David! Like Dad, he too had become king! Maybe Absalom should have been king. After all, he had training in war. Oops, Abe was dead. All right, what about Amnon? Yeah, right! Absalom killed him. Adonijah! Yes, Adonijah should be king. He had already crowned himself king. What's more? He already had the support of the top army generals and the pastor of the federal republic, or should we say kingdom? Nope! Dad insisted that Jedidiah should become king. What was he supposed to do now? He did not have Dad's pedigree, he did not have Dad's men, he did not have Dad's strength, and he did not have Dad's experience. Whoa! He had nothing! To make matters worse, he was just a boy!

He needed something. If he was going to keep the kingdom the way Dad left it, he needed to have all Dad had. Or better still, he needed something that would encapsulate all that Dad had.

Guess what!

He got it!

Not the strength, not the men, not the experience, and not the pedigree, but something else. Something Dad did not have the luxury of, but it could match all that Dad had and more. It was given to him on a platter of gold; it was given to him in excess.

It was unrivaled wisdom and extreme understanding!

Nothing could confuse him; he had answers to every puzzle. His father dazzled kings with strength, but Jedidiah amazed queens (especially, and kings, of course) with his wisdom and understanding. His father built the kingdom with a grand display of raw power; but Jedidiah sustained the kingdom with a grand exhibition of understanding and wisdom. All that his father got with a sword, he got with a pen. His wisdom matched and surpassed his Dad's strength.

So let me introduce the new greatest king of the world to you.

His name?

King Solomon Jedidiah Ben-David!

He became great not with a sword or strength but with a pen and understanding wisdom.

The kind of wisdom he received was almost infinite. God said, "I have given you a wise heart plus an understanding heart. None before you have received such, and none after you can receive such!"

Wow! That was almost definitely infinite. So bring it on—the hard questions, the confusing matters, the hard judgments, tough puzzles, mind-rattling wonders, the works—and watch Solomon demystify them.

People traveled from far and wide to listen to him. Wondering how far? Sheba traveled all the way from East Africa to hear him! Royalties came to hear him talk. No wonder they could not fight with him. They all wanted to hear him. People went on to research difficult questions to ask him; people must have tried to trip him up. But every time, he always had an answer. He had answers to every war strategy; he had a solution to every medical ailment. When enemies came and tried to cut off the food and water supply and lay ambush at the gate, he had a solution. There was nothing, absolutely nothing, that could confuse him.

At least not until that fateful day!

Somebody asked a question, and guess what the answer was! Solomon, wise King Jedidiah Solomon Ben-David, answered, "I am confused." Understanding Solomon said, "I don't understand."

What could it have been? What on earth could have confused this all-wise king? I bet kings of other kingdoms would have been so shocked. I bet they would have called their generals together to plot an assault on this one point! What could it have been? Could that have been his weakness?

"Three things amaze me, no, four things I'll never understand.[b]"

That is rather too sincere. Not one, not two, not three, but four things! He said three things then changed his mind and said four. Why? Was it a style of writing? Was he trying to emphasize something? Or was he too ashamed to acknowledge the fact that the fourth item was confusing. Was there something about the fourth thing that he did not want to talk about? Maybe he couldn't understand why he didn't understand it. Maybe it was the key to his weakness. Maybe revealing it would mean revealing too much. Maybe saying it would mean exposing his kingdom. He said, "Three things amaze me ..." and then as an afterthought added, "no, four ..." What were these three things? What was the fourth thing that was so difficult to say?

"How an eagle flies so high in the sky, how a snake glides over a rock, how a ship navigates the ocean ..."[c]

Was it that? That's understandable. Come to think of it, with all the technology available, nobody can still tell us how an eagle flies so high. All we have are set of speculative grammar and mathematical formulas. We know why, but nobody still knows how!

A snake has no legs. It has a very slippery belly. So tell me, how does a slippery-bellied snake move on a slippery rock surface? We may know why, but how? That's still a mystery. You know it yourself; you know how difficult it is for you to climb a rock barefooted. But imagine a snake slithering with speed across a slippery rocky surface.

The ship! Yes, of course. We have heard all the laws; we have been able to find out why it is possible for a ship to move and navigate the ocean. We know why it can stay afloat, but how?

The *why* question requires remote-cause answers. The *how* question requires a foundational-cause answer! Everybody, at least most, can answer why; but nobody—not you, not me, not the intelligent scientists of today, not even wise Solomon—could answer it. So even though it is surprising, it is very understandable that Solomon could not answer for those three things. Even the person that asked must have said something like, "Well, thank goodness he is not God. At least he doesn't know everything!" So they couldn't have, I can't, and I don't think you can blame him for not knowing the answer to those three puzzles. In fact, we should appreciate his sincerity.

But there is something else. Yes, the fourth piece of the puzzle. The very one he found difficult to mention. What could it be?

"And the way of a man with a maid.[d]"

"A man making his way with a virgin.[e]"

"And a man and a woman falling in love.[f]"

"The growth of love between a man and a girl.[g]"

Aha! I knew it was going to be something! But back up a little. What is so confusing about a man and woman in love? There is nothing confusing about it. In fact, Solomon had no problems with a man in love with a woman. He wrote a whole book narrating the love between a man and a woman. The Song of Songs, popularly called the Song of Solomon, was written as a tribute to the beautiful feeling called love. He called it the Song of Songs; he exalted it above the songs of David called the psalms. David was an expert in worship, but he was an expert, a professor, of love. So as far as he knew, his song was greater than any other. Maybe because of the amount of research he did before writing the Song of Songs. He was Solomon, the wisest man on earth for God's sake. He knew about love. He understood the subject. So what was confusing was not love; it was not a man loving a woman. Watch carefully what he said confused him.

"And **the way** of a man with a maiden."
"And **the way** of a man with a girl."
"And a man and a woman **falling** in love."
"The **growth of love** between a man and a girl."

Did you get that? He talked about the "way"! He talked about the "falling"! He talked about the "growth"! He was talking about a process!

Two people from different backgrounds, with different principles and policies and upbringings and lifestyles, two people with absolutely nothing in common, suddenly come together and begin to live together, and they actually agree to become one! Why? They attribute it to love. What actually happened to them? Why did they drop all the differences? Why the sudden change? Why do they suddenly become vulnerable to each other? Love, love they say. What happens to a man and a woman when they become lovers? This same question baffled Solomon the wise. We can attempt to answer it, but let me put it straight to you: it confused Solomon then and it will confuse you now! So don't get it twisted!

Wise King Solomon was also confused asking this same question. He talked about "the way of a man with a maiden"!

The Hebrew word translated "man" in this passage is *geber*, and it means a valiant man; a warrior. *Al-maw* is the Hebrew for "maiden," and it means a young lady, a virgin.

Solomon was saying he did not understand what force was so strong as to make a warrior fall flat before a young lady!

This is not about spirituality, it is not about how much Scripture you know, and it is now about how many hours you spend praying. It is about a force that does not respect you! It is this same force that destroyed the kingdom of Solomon, the very kingdom that was built by the strength of David and sustained by the wisdom of Solomon!

It finds its way into the carnal and the spiritual alike. Solomon in all his wisdom could not fathom it. The biggest problem with us is that we try to cage it, we try to master it. It has proven its strength over and over again in the lives of strong men. It has an endless list of mighty men that it has brought under. We know it, we feel it, but sadly, we trivialize it.

Don't be so surprised!

Emotions!

Yes, that's what it is called!

When a man loves a woman, emotions begin to develop. Many times, it grows until it takes charge!

We have defined emotions in so many ways. Some have called it a deep feeling of care; others say it is passion. Some believe emotions to be sentimental. One truth though that everyone would agree with is that emotions are a controlling force. It is the one thing that makes us vulnerable to someone. It is the one thing that makes us let down the curtain. It is the one thing that makes us restless. Imagine yourself getting jealous because some guy is chatting with your fiancée! That would never have happened before emotions came in!

Such a good thing, emotions! It is such a wonderful gift. Do you realize we serve an emotional God? He said, "I your God am a jealous God"! It is this emotional nature of God that makes him go out of his way to help. It is the same emotions that make him hurt so badly when we make a mess of his grace!

Such a strange thing, emotions! Emotion it is that has made many people lose grip of their lives and principles. A lot of people have found themselves in very compromising situations. Things that ordinarily would not happen can now happen. Emotions are tender feelings that make us vulnerable to our deepest weaknesses.

Properly written, emotions are *e-motion*, energy in motion. It is an energy source that wells up in us, seeking to power our actions. A proper understanding of this energy can help us subdue its hold to a very considerable extent.

What then is this energy in motion?

Story Time

Memoirs of a blind man![h]

"Aaaaaarrrrgggggghhhhh! God no, no, this can't be happening to me. Where is my strength?" That was the cry that went out of my lips when I discovered that six strong men had bound me and were gouging out my eyes. Ordinarily, they would have been no problem, but now my strength was gone. If I could turn the hands of time, I would not repeat the mistake I made. Oh, what a grievous mistake, one I would forever regret. You may wonder what my complaint is all about, but if you have tasted the kind of power I had and then see yourself in chains working in the prison mill, then you most definitely would understand. I was strong. How painful it is that I now refer to my strength in past tenses.

I had unusual strength. People called me a god because of the extraordinary things I could do. I had no soldiers fighting with me; I was just one man that was enough to win the war! There was this one time I got really angry because my father-in-law had given my wife to my best man. I was so angry that I went into the forest and caught three hundred jackals, tied their tails in pairs, tied a fire torch to their tails, and sent them into the field of the elders of the city. This sparked annoyance among the people. The soldiers took my wife and her father and burned them at a stake. That just annoyed me even more. I went out and single-handedly killed many of those soldiers. Again, my action sparked a fit of anger among the men in the military. They were so angry; they threatened to destroy my family.

My brothers came to me at the cave of Etam, where I had gone to cool off. They begged me to go with them. What I did not know was that they had made a deal with my enemies to turn me in. They tied me with brand-new ropes and took me to Lehi, where the soldiers were waiting to tear me from limb to limb. The trouble here was that Lehi was a town with flat lands, unlike Etam that was hilly. I preferred Etam because it always gave me an advantage any time I was under attack. Now at Lehi, I knew I needed extra help, more so because I was faced with about a thousand enemies who wanted to put me down by all means.

The Philistines, for that was what my enemies were called, came at me with all sorts of weapons, shouting at the top of their lungs in victory. I was one man with hands tied behind his back, tied with brand-new, terribly strong ropes. What was I to do? I then began to roar like a man possessed by some strange spirit. Without efforts, I broke the ropes that bound me and charged toward them. Without looking, I picked the nearest thing my hands could find as a weapon and madly fought my way through the men. After about forty minutes of endless shouting and fighting, I was standing in a pool of dead men. I had killed a thousand men with the jawbone of an ass!

It was feats like this that made people call me a god. But I knew that it was much more. Nobody knew, but I had a secret I was supposed to protect with my life. You see, I was born in very mysterious circumstances. My parents had waited for a very long time for a child. When I finally came, they made it their responsibility to protect me. At my birth, my parents were given instructions on how to raise me. There were certain laws I was to keep and secrets I was to guard with my life. My parents always told me that my great strength came from those laws I was told to keep. Although some of the laws were strange, I had to do as I was told. For example, I was not supposed to take alcohol, but most importantly, I was not to let any razor touch my head. So though people saw me as a god, I knew the secret of my strength, and I knew it was supposed to be a secret till the day of my death.

I faced armies countless times, I fought a lion with my bare hands and killed it, and I even carried the gate of a city up a mountain.

Nothing was ever able to stand in my way. I always came out of every battle unscathed. I was a god, at least till I met her.

Her name was Delilah. Oh, what a day it was that I met her. I happened upon her on my way from a slaughter. She was struggling with three giant men who were looking to steal some of the sheep she was watering. I thought she was brave, because even though she looked smallish, she ran around the men, grabbing from them what she could. I had laughed really hard before stepping in to help her. After dislodging the men, I picked her up with one arm and carried her all the way home. We were instantly in love. Even though she was a Philistine and closely connected with my sworn enemies, I loved her dearly. That was the beginning of my journey from endless power to a life of endless punishments.

It had started after about six months of living blissfully together. She had come home late that evening and was asking all sorts of questions. She wanted to know where I got my strength. At first, I thought it was one of those romantic jokes she was playing, so I played along. I told her my power would be taken away from me if I were tied with new bowstrings. I was surprised when she came home the next day with new bowstrings. She had tied me securely. After a while of pretending to struggle, she called out, "Hey, Samson, the Philistines are here." Without efforts and without even thinking, I had broken the bowstrings and was looking for the nearest thing my hands could find. I was ready to shed some more Philistine blood.

Delilah was angry because I wasn't telling her the real truth. I didn't see why she needed to know, and I was determined not to tell her a secret I was to take to my grave.

My decision not to tell took the peace from me. She did not stop and would not take no for an answer. She molested me daily, prodding for an answer to her question. I was in shock because for the second time in my life, I felt helpless. All I had done to put her off had failed. I told her to tie me with new strings. She did. I even got close to the truth when I told her to weave the locks of my hair into the fabrics on the loom. But every time she did, she found out that I was not telling the truth, because when she called out to me about the arrival of the Philistines, I shook off all the ties and weaved with so much ease. I did not know what to do anymore. I loved her, but she was beginning to doubt it. She claimed I didn't trust her; she even said I was toying with her just as a cat does a mouse. It was too hard to see her in such a state. I was helplessly confused. The first time I felt helpless, it was a secret that was also arm-twisted out of me.

I had just gotten married to my first wife and was hosting friends at a seven-day long feast. On the first day, I gave them a riddle with the promise of a new wardrobe of clothes to whoever got the answer. The penalty for not getting to answer within the seven-day period was a new wardrobe from them to me. On the fifth day, my wife came whining to me about the fact that I refused to tell the answer to my riddle. In her words, "Samson, you hate me. You don't love me. You gave a riddle to my people, but you won't even tell me the answer." What was I to do? I hated being helpless, but somehow, it felt like I was losing the war. When I refused to tell her, she turned on the tears for the remaining days of the feast. So by the seventh day, I was finally defeated. I couldn't believe the words were coming out of my mouth when I was telling her the riddle and its answer! She ended up telling the answer to her friends, who ripped me off!

Being in that same spot again, one would think I had learned my lesson. But I just did not know what to do. Delilah had gotten me; I was between a rock and a hard place. I knew it was wrong to tell her; I knew she probably had some sinister motive, but it was as though I was under a spell. For the second time in my life, I lost a battle. I told her that truth. I told her that since birth, no razor had touched my hair. I told her that cutting of my seven locks would spell my doom. I tried my best to fight it, but I lost.

She made me fall asleep on her lap, and with a razor, she cut off my locks. I felt it. I felt my strength drain off. And when, as before, she called out to me that the Philistines were here, I could do nothing. I was just another man with a lot of muscles.

I have been in this dungeon for two whole years, grinding in pain and darkness as I work the mill. I hear the shouts. I hear the taunts. Even fellow prisoners speak of me with derision. They mock the fact that I was brought down by a smallish woman. I hear the stories; I hear of Delilah, how she got wealthy from bringing me to my kneels.

Alone with my thoughts in the darkness of blindness, I keep going over that day. Though my locks have grown back to place, I know it will never be the same again.

I fought and killed a lion with my bare hands, but I could not defeat two tiny women!

I killed a thousand men in forty minutes with the jawbone of an ass, but I could not defeat one smallish woman in six months!

The Philistines were terrified of me, but I was terrified by a young lady!

I could lift her off the ground with one hand; she could lift me off my senses with her tears!

I had the strength of a god, but it took her nothing to ruin me!

The great Samson was brought down by smallish Delilah!

What happened to me?

This same question baffled Solomon the wise. We can attempt to answer it, but let me put it straight to you: it confused Solomon then and it will confuse you now! So don't get it twisted!

This is not about spirituality. It is not about how much Scripture you know or how many hours you spend praying. It is about a force that does not respect you! It is this same force that destroyed the kingdom of Solomon, the very kingdom that was built by the strength of David and sustained by the wisdom of Solomon!

Energy in Motion

Every day, we experience emotions in one form or the other. We see emotions all around us. From our homes to our place of work and back, emotions light up the way like street lamps on a dark night. One may wonder why we have emotions, seeing all that is done as a result of them. I believe emotions are the means by which we make sense of our world, and react to it. I will give some examples of actions born out of emotion.

- Workers holding placards and marching on the streets while demanding better work conditions.
- A roughly dressed man holding scattered files but running to work.
- A bunch of teens throwing their high school graduation caps into the air.
- An eighty-five-year-old woman holding flowers at the graveside of her dead husband.
- A mother dashing toward the hospital on hearing her son was involved in an accident.
- A father running, arms opened wide, toward his daughter standing at the doorway.

Emotions! We see them every day, everywhere, and every time. A large fraction of the actions we take and the things we do is fueled by emotions. The reason behind every action is traceable to some emotional interaction of the mind. Emotions have made people do some really good things; others have found themselves doing some really sick things as a result of emotions.

Have you ever been angry?

Have you ever felt embarrassed?

Have you ever felt aroused?

Have you ever been disappointed?

It was your emotions speaking. We may try, but we would almost never succeed to get rid of our emotions, for they are what make us uniquely human. The problem though is that many people have let their emotion get the better of them. A lot of very sick things go on in our world because some people have allowed their emotions to run amok.

Given the fact that emotions tend to control the way we act and behave, it is very possible for us to act in ways that would even surprise us. It is of great importance therefore to understand the dynamics of emotions, so we can, to a very wise degree, control our actions.

Now there is a tricky twist to our emotions—they can enter a gyrated state of hyper action!

What happens when a man meets a likeable woman? What happens when two people are in love?

High-tension emotion happens!

With the involvement of the opposite sex, all our emotions enter a hyperactive state, especially when the person catches our fancy. Everything ranging from affection to jealousy to anger becomes excitedly hyperactive.

So imagine all the ways you would respond ordinarily to issues, and then multiply that by a lot. Now you know how you would respond to those same issues when *love* enters the picture. It was this realization that made our wise king raise his hands in utter bewilderment when faced with the relationship between a man and a woman.[a] Have you not wondered why men suddenly begin to act strange when they are in love? Have you not seen women throw tantrums because their friends made misplaced comments about their husbands? It is the high-tension wire of emotions.

Before you *fell* in love, you did not bother who he hung out with, but now, like an eagle, you monitor his movement and complain about his "miniskirt-wearing" secretary! It is because both of you have gone into an emotional lock.

Apart from the overprotective nature of love emotions, there is also the overactive nature. People in love, especially those just starting out, seem very touchy around their loved ones. They get easily upset; they get offended by things that ordinarily would have meant nothing. The questions I find many people asking are these:

- "Why is it that the person I love the most is also the person I am capable of hurting the most?
- "Why is it that love can in one instant turn to hate?
- "Why does it *feel* like I don't love him anymore?

Love and Emotions

In the opening chapters, we established the fact that love was totally different from feelings. Feeling, that is what emotions are. When we take a critical look at the mistake a lot of people have made in their lives, we see it goes down to confusing emotions for love.

I will illustrate with yet another true story.

Helen had just had her heart ripped out by Tom, who she had been dating for about a year. She had really been in love with him, but unfortunately, things did not seem to work out. She had invested a lot of emotions in that relationship. Now for some unjustifiable reason, Tom wanted out. She was devastated and shattered. In this dark and lonely time of her life, there was Joe.

Joe was her friend from school. He felt deeply concerned for his friend, so he decided to cheer her up and help her through this rough patch in her life. He was up and around, helping her with stuff and taking her out just to make sure he brightened her mood. Each time they were out, Helen would share with him heartrending tales of how broken her heart was and how lucky she was to have him helping her. Joe could empathize with her. Somehow, he could relate with what she was going through. He discovered that he was spending most of his time with her, thinking about ways he could make her happy. He found himself wishing there was something he could do to make her feel better. As time went on, Joe found himself contemplating whether or not to start a romantic relationship with Helen.

By now, we know that an emotional knot formed between Joe and Helen. The important question though is this: was it *love* that was making Joe consider a romantic relationship with Helen or just his feeling of pity and empathy?

Between a man and a woman, there is a great force of connection that is usually mistaken for love. The emotion, affection, is usually mistaken for love. But truth be told, affection is simply fondness, not love.

Love, being a verb, is a decision to be *responsible* and *involved* with the life of another person despite and in spite all that may happen. But like established already, the introduction of love heightens activity of emotions. Therefore, emotions act as grease making love fluid and organic. Understanding this difference between love and affection, which is an emotion, helps us pinpoint the real reason behind the butterfly feeling in our stomach. Love is a decision that we can abide by, but emotions are fleeting; they are here today and gone tomorrow.

From the story above, if Joe makes a decision to start a relationship with Helen because he *feels* pity for her, he would be left with nothing after all the dust of her hard time settles.

How many marriages have ended in divorce because all the excitement had died off?

How many promises of a "happily ever after" life have suddenly turned to a "sadly ever after" life?

You see, that is the biggest problem with our emotions. It is a controlling force that wants to be the basis of all our decisions. When one is truly in love, the emotions are multiplied to make it easy to do all that love demands and entails, but even at that, making decisions and taking actions should be a process of logically thinking through all the options instead of acting on the spur of the moment. This is because affection is not the only emotion at play; affection is not the only emotion struggling for attention. Every one of us has an emotional tank, an emotional tank that is hyperactive.

The Emotional Tank

Imagine a huge containing vessel with a lot of emotional particles bouncing around. That would be you!

We are all equally capable of love and hate, sorrow, and joy; apathy and empathy; and embarrassment and ecstasy. The odd twist, though, is when a person of the opposite sex is involved and all these emotions get hyperactive together. Therefore, it is easy to get terribly angry with someone you terribly love. Have you not wondered why you are hurt the most by the one you love the most? It is simple because your *feelings* of love and hurt are all bundled together in your hyperactive emotional tank.

Emotions abound all the time, but they get extra active when interest is developed in the opposite sex. It is this state of the emotions we are interested in. The emotions displayed are usually not only directed at the object of attraction but to everything and everyone that is involved or that interferes. A man could become violent just because some random guy is flirting with the lady he *loves*. Between the two lovers, desires are heightened, and when those desires are not met, frustration becomes the dominant emotion.

At every given point, depending on the state of affairs between the two people in love, a particular emotion plays a dominant role. For example, when everything is going well, affection and its attendant desires are at the top of the tank. When things go badly, guilt, anger, frustration, disappointment, and one of the many negative emotions rule the joint. It is important to note that emotions are fleeting and can be in constant change.

For two people in love, the fondness and affection shared between them comes with its attending desires. There is the desire to be together all the time, the desire for communication, the desire for expression, and yes, the desire for physical intimacy. And so, even though at the beginning of the courtship, you decided not to toy with your bodies, you find this strange force pulling you closer and closer to the point where you are inevitably doing what you agreed not to do. It is the controlling force of emotion.

Let me illustrate this point with another true story.

Emma and Peter had it going very well in their relationship. They had Pastor Johnson counseling them when things went awry. But then, six months in, Emma was feeling really uncomfortable with the state of things. She felt things were not going as agreed. She was contemplating a break up. According to her, "The relationship was taking me away from God." Although she did not tell Pastor Johnson what was really going on, he knew. He knew that the emotion of guilt was taking center stage. And just as he thought, Emma and Peter were already beginning to experiment with their bodies. Although they enjoyed it at the time, the aftertaste was one of guilt. Not able to stand the guilt anymore, Emma wanted out.

Let's analyze the play of emotions in this story.

The affections and heightened level of need made them want to get more intimate—they began playing with their bodies. The knowledge of what was right compared with what they were doing made Emma feel guilty, so she wanted out.

I have seen this story played out many times. I have watched many happy soon-to-be-wed couples break up simply because they could not handle the heat and tension emotions brought their way during their courtship. We would all lead happier lives if we learned how to make decisions in the heat of emotions.

Standing the Heat

It is possible to make the right decisions even in the heat of passion and over flooding emotions. It is possible to stand for what is right. I am sure you agree that some of the huge problems we face in relationships and marriages stem from the fact that we let our emotions fly off the handle. We take decisions on the spur of the moment without thinking things through and receiving proper counsel. In the opening story of this book, I told about Cynthia who planned to get married as a virgin but had ended up on the wrong side of the road. Truth is she missed the boat when she failed to realize the hold her emotions were beginning to have on her. Like her, a lot of people have broken their wedding vows. The story was told of a young executive who had a very dutiful secretary. She always made sure his schedule was well organized. As he spent more time at work than home, she filled his life more than his wife did. He began to have revenge sex with his wife. Revenge sex is the kind you have when you are angry that you could not have sex with somebody else. Tell me how long it would take for him to fall for the obvious direction his emotions are leading to.

Today's world is sex driven. The movies, the billboards, the news, even the prevailing fashion, spell sex in bold letters. Everyone seems to be all too aware of the prevailing hold passion has on people; therefore, it has become a weapon. Many young Christians are in the fight of their lives while trying to stay sane in a world where it is considered insane to wait till marriage for sex. The war between decision and desires has never been hotter.

I submit today though that it is possible to make the right decisions even in the heat of passion and over flooding emotions. It is possible to stand for what is right. The following steps are simple but very helpful in your quest to taming your emotions.

1. Decide to be in control. This sounds very easy, but it is usually the most difficult step to take. We usually make decisions but without the biting zeal to see it through.

2. Be truthful to yourself. Like the old me, a lot of people are overconfident. While there is nothing wrong with being confident, there is everything wrong with deliberately refusing to recognize the dangers that lie on the path. Emotions are a very powerful force that wants to control our actions. That is a truth you must tell yourself.

3. Don't just decide; *make* the decision. It is easier said than done. Usually, when we find ourselves in a dark place, we immediately take the first idea that pops into our minds. But to tame that emotional pull, you must be able to slow down to create a decision. Remember the story of Esau? He

was hungry, and without thinking, he decided to sell off his birthright for a plate of food.[b] Remember Joseph? He *made* a decision not to put Mary to public disgrace despite the fact that all the evidence pointed an accusing finger at her.[c] Don't just decide; think things through and *make* the decision.

4. Turn off the gas. Anybody that plays with fire would get burned. Walk away from situations that ignite the fire of your emotions. Emotions by nature are meant to be expressed and not bottled up. It is no use bottling up your emotions and trying to manage them. Turn the knob and put out the fire. Pack your bags and flee the scene of emotional activation.

5. Get a confidant. Because by nature emotions are not meant to be bottled up, you need to ensure they are poured out. To avoid pouring them out wrongly, get a mature and trusted friend to pour your heart to.

6. God is ready to help too. Don't leave him out of the picture, because in the final analysis, it's his help that counts for the most.

<u>Story Time</u>

Lovesick![d]

He was breathing hard like one who had just completed a one-hundred-meter dash. Indeed, he had just completed a dash, a very scintillating one at that. He entered the race not to win the Olympics but to win her heart. Now he didn't know if it was worth it. As he lay on the bed feeling the warmth of her flesh against his body, his mind raced back into time.

It started on his twenty-first birthday. His father, the king, had thrown a huge party to celebrate his son's entrance into the world of men. He had proven his mettle before the nation's army chiefs.

As the king's son turning twenty-one, he had to prove he was worthy of his father's throne. There were a series of competitions organized to prove him. There was the sword fight, the target precision, and the goliath fight. The goliath fight was especially interesting. That was because his father, King David, had killed a giant as a youth to prove his mettle to the king. A few days leading to the competition, the strongest of the king's men stole into enemy territory to kidnap a fearsome-looking troll of a giant. It was this giant that the king's son would face. It was a battle to the death.

Amnon had trained every day since he was eighteen. The day had finally come. He knew he had to put up all his best. Armed with words of wisdom and encouragement from his father and the joint chiefs, and with the promise of endless rewards and glory, he marched out amidst the claps and shouts of the people who had by now thronged the palace's Victory Square. He marched out tall and handsome and confident.

He was a troll indeed; the giant was really fearsome. When the bell went for the battle to start, all that could be heard were grunts and clangs of swords; all that could be seen were bodies tangled in sweat and blood. Then at last, the prince emerged from the dust with the giant's head in his hands. He had proven himself! He had brought down a giant! He was now officially a man worthy of the throne.

King David was delighted that his firstborn son had been able to prove his worth; he decided not to go easy on the celebration. He invited kings from neighboring countries; he also invited the best jesters in the entire realm. His son was going to enter the league of extraordinary men in grand style.

At the party, Amnon and his friends had the best of things, ranging from food to drinks to entertainers, and even to women. Everything they needed became available at the snap of the finger. It was at this time, when he was at the height of fun, he saw her.

Tamar was a tall, beautiful, and slender lady who had been trained in the ways and manners befitting a princess, for that was who she was. She had royal blood flowing through her veins, for she was the daughter of King David and Maachah, who was the daughter of Talmai, king of Geshur. She was an excellent example of royalty. She walked it, dressed it, talked it, and felt it. Her grace was just simply ravishing.

She had been put in charge of the king's chamberlains at Amnon's party. She ensured that the king and his visitors had their cups and plates always full of the best and freshest stock. In the course of carrying out her duties, she had come to ask Amnon and his friends if they needed anything. It was then he saw her.

Of course, Amnon knew Tamar; she was his half-sister. He had always seen her in the palace, even though he had not closely related with her. But he thought there was something different about the way she looked that night. Probably it was because she was not wearing the long-sleeved robe that virgin daughters of the king usually wore. Probably it was because of the grace with which she gave orders to the servants. Whatever it was, Amnon was hooked! He knew it was wrong for him to think of his half-sister in this way, and the knowledge was killing him. He had left the party before it was time for the king to officially present him with the prince's scepter of authority. Nothing seemed to make sense to him anymore. He had seen a jewel, and like a spoiled child, he was determined to have it.

For one week, Amnon walked around the palace with his head bowed and low, thinking and wondering what he was going to do. He had not eaten any decent food since his party; his mind was full of thoughts; thoughts directed toward Tamar. He had devised means to get close to her, but all his efforts hit the rocks. His biggest obstacle was the imposing presence of his immediate younger half-brother, Absalom.

Absalom was the brother of Tamar, and like an eagle, he protected his sister from the preening eyes of men who were beginning to take notice of her stunning beauty. As a young man, Absalom was the personification of royalty. Though he had not yet competed for the right to the throne, everyone could easily see him becoming the next king. He was smart and courageous, but beyond that, he was handsome and graceful. He was popularly thought to be the most handsome of the king's sons. He usually let his hair grow all year. When cut, it became a priceless gift. Such was the shared fortune of beauty Absalom and his sister, Tamar, had. Apart from the fact that he was a threat to Amnon's throne, he also had a quiet and distant look that made him quite unpredictable.

Amnon felt a heavy knot in his stomach. His desire for Tamar and the throne was under the threat of his *younger* brother. With his constant worrying and lack of food, Amnon had fallen sick—lovesick.

Jonadab, Amnon's closest friend, had almost given up on him. He wondered why a man who could get any lady he wanted would go on and on about a lady living under the same roof with him. He had nudged his friend to just go ahead and have Tamar, but the situation had only gotten worse. That was why, when he got the king's message, he was irritated.

King David was worried about the strange behavior of his son. He had expected him to be happy and exuberant, but instead, his giant-killing son was going around the palace like a dog that had been drenched in the rain. He had made several attempts to reach out to his son without success. When he was told of Amnon's sickness, he had frustratingly sent for Jonadab, Amnon's closest friend.

Jonadab had the best idea. He had devised a plan that would end the show of shame Amnon had put up. He got Amnon to make his father, the king, ask Tamar to help prepare his favorite meal and help feed him. The king, of course, gave the necessary instructions.

Amnon had sprung out of his bed the moment he heard the click of the door's lock. He had grabbed Tamar from behind, begging her to sleep with him. He did not care for anything else anymore; he had forgotten about the throne and about the fact that she was his sister. All he was interested in, all that existed in his world, was her. So, despite her plea, he forced himself on her.

Once it was over, he grabbed his robe and sat up on the bed, not wanting to have anything to do with her. *What is so special about her?* he wondered. *Why did I stoop so low?* Thinking about how much he had lost in the past week, his heart filled with hate for her. And like a raving mad man, he screamed at the top of his lungs, "Get out, whore!"

He hated her in a proportion greater than the "love" he had had for her. He hated her because, as fragile as she was, she had made him let go of his sense of direction. He thought he would be proud of the fact that he was able to conquer her, but he realized that he was the one who was conquered. He hated himself; he hated her.

Tamar was in tears. She couldn't believe what had happened to her; all her carefulness and grace stolen away in an instant. If it were some random guy, it would have hurt less. But her brother!

With tears flowing freely, she begged Amnon. "Please don't send me away. Sending me away is worse than raping me." She sobbed, but her pleas fell on deaf ears as Amnon got his servant to throw out the princess.

Emotions are huge forces that develop when a man is attracted to a woman.

Even giant killers can be brought to their knees by it.

Your emotion can lead you down the wrong path, even when you intended to take the right one.

Emotion is not equal to love.

A person controlled by emotion switches easily between love and hate.

Like Amnon …

- We see the beautiful lady and our emotions take the driver seat!
- We shut down our reason and do as our emotions bid!
- W forget all our goals and concentrate on an ephemeral pursuit!
- We drop our swords and give out our hearts to be torn to shreds!

The Atmosphere You Permit ...

Hannah, twenty-five, and Bob, twenty-four, were members of the same church. They were both active workers and dedicated Christians. In less than two weeks after they were introduced, they became friends. They talked about general issues, did their Bible studies together, and prayed often. As time went on, they began to feel closer to each other. Hannah openly confessed to Bob that she had *fallen* in love with him. Bob knew it was true, because he was also in love with her. Bob had a few considerations, though. Although he did not mind being in love with a lady that was older than him, he was already in a relationship with somebody else. They talked about it and agreed that starting a relationship was not going to be a good idea; they both thought they could handle their feelings. But with the progress of time, as their trust for each other grew, so did the feelings and emotions. They became quite attached to each other. One night, Bob was stranded from work and needed a place to pass the night. The only person he trusted enough to call was Hannah. He spent the night at Hannah's place. By the time it was morning, they had barely escaped having sex.

Becky and Andrew were members of the same student body in their university. They were in charge of the student body's newsletters, magazines, and general publications. They were also members of the same Christian fellowship. They were friends, casual friends. Toward of the end of the semester, as was customary, they published a magazine containing important articles describing the issues and important events that had happened during the semester. The process of publishing the magazine was challenging. Although there were other members on the editorial board, both of them worked closely together. They gathered the articles, decided on the process of editing, even worked on the marketing plan together. As they worked together, they grew attached to each other, and soon the feelings they had for each other were rocket high. Becky was wary of her feelings because she did not know Andrew well enough to start a romantic relationship with him. Apart from working together, they did not actually have any other thing in common. She thought it was wise to take it slowly. After working hard together for six weeks, the magazine was finally ready to hit the press. She decided to visit Andrew's house to celebrate their success. They talked and played for a long time until it got dark. By morning, Becky was in tears.

Nathan and Lisa were in love; they were to be married in few months. You could tell from the way they acted around each other that their love tank was full. Added to their rich love for each other was their love for God. They both loved God and were in active service for him. Nathan was a pastor and Lisa was the director of her church's choir. The trouble with them was that their church responsibilities were so daunting that they did not have a lot of time to spend together. So any time they were together, they utilized it to the fullest. Lisa lived with her parents and her four other siblings. Any time Nathan came to visit, she always insisted on going to her room so they could have all the time and privacy needed to discuss their plans, etc. Nathan soon discovered that every time they were alone, a *magical* force was pulling him toward her. He knew he wanted to do so many evil things. He made several attempts, attempts that were vehemently rebuffed by Lisa. The question he asked was, "Why do I lose control?"

What do these stories have in common? What would you say happened?

In the preceding chapters, we talked about mistakes that abound in relationships between people of the opposite sex. A lot of these mistakes happen because we carelessly overlook the tiny bits that make up the final structure. But knowing the theory of a subject doesn't make us experts. A lot of people know the right thing, and as is the case in some of the stories I have shared, want to do the right thing. But they still find the right thing elusive. They still find themselves in the very same mess they promised not to get into. Take addicts, for instance. How many times do they weep and cry because of what the addiction does to them and their loved ones? How many times do they promise never to go back to it? How many times do they clear out all the addictive elements they've got locked up in their closets? But how many times do you find them back to square one? The truth is that knowing the truth and doing the truth are two totally different things. It takes the will and desire to know, to really know the truth, but I submit that it takes much more than sheer will and desire to put what you know into action.

Several questions spring up from the above stories. For example, why did Bob, even though he did not want to start a relationship with Hannah, find himself almost having sex with her? Why did Hannah, being a Christian lady that wanted to wait till she was married, almost throw it all off to Bob?

Why did Becky find herself in an untoward situation with Andrew, even though she was sure she did not trust him?

Why did Pastor Nathan lose control?

I am sure you have answers to these questions. I am also sure you will refer to previous chapters of this book for you answers. The answers to those questions have already been discussed in detail, save one.

The point at which all your resolve becomes useless is the point at which you do the unthinkable. It is the point where you break your vow, where you go back on your words, where you return to the addiction, where you not just let down your standard but where you dump it. You only reach that point when the atmosphere is right.

The Atmosphere You Permit Determines What You Commit

The rain falls when the atmosphere is saturated. Action matches intention when the atmosphere permits it. Before anyone gets to the point where he does the unthinkable, he would have done that same thing over and over in his heart already. But before the action in his heart matches the physical action, the atmosphere must be right. That is the reason why a lot of people only realize what they have done after the deed. The saturated atmosphere is the point where your resolve is no longer in control. Your emotions take the driver seat, and despite what you *know*, you seem not to be able to stop yourself.

In the preceding chapter, we talked about not letting emotions control your actions. We also talked about the importance of *making* decisions before taking action. As true as all those things are, they are only valid outside the wrong atmosphere. No wonder the Bible says to abstain from all *appearance* of evil.[a] In order words, do not go into the atmosphere that will cause evil!

What are these atmospheres we must refuse to permit? Let's take a quick look at them right away!

Mental Atmosphere

The most difficult part of our bodies to tame is the mind. A lot of people have mastered their bodies; they could do very amazing things with those bodies, but the mind? The mind has huge control over our actions. The things we think about ultimately become the things we do. No wonder the Bible says to keep vigilant watch of our hearts, for that's where life starts.[b] Truth be told, a lot of Christians have their minds messed up with evil thoughts. More and more young Christians are being tied in the web of pornography. Tell me: how do you hope to maintain your resolve to honor the marriage bed when your mind is already full of horrific and explicit sexual imagery? The mind is fed by the eyes and the ears majorly. So what are the things you enjoy seeing or reading? What are the things you enjoy listening to? It was this realization that made Job make a covenant with himself; he said he would never undress a girl with his eyes.[c] The atmosphere created in the mind paves the way for the physical action to occur. Remember that every sin begins with a thought. A man is not different from his thoughts, for as he thinks in his heart, so is he.[d]

Summing it all up, friends, I'd say you'll do best by filling your minds and meditating on things true, noble, reputable, authentic, compelling, gracious—the best, not the worst; the beautiful, not the ugly; things to praise, not things to curse.[e]

Uttered Atmosphere

We live in a world where there is freedom of speech. Everybody can say anything anyhow and anywhere. But I bet you know that the words of our mouths shape our lives. The words we say are an outward representation of what we think on the inside. You don't get wormy apples off a healthy tree nor good apples off a diseased tree. The health of the apple tells the health of the tree. You must begin with your own life-giving lives. It's who you are, not what you say and do, that counts. Your true being brims over into true words and deeds.[f] When you are all the time talking about things that connote evil, you are with your tongue manipulating the environment around you. You may not even be speaking evil things; it could be things that are unnecessarily suggestive or inappropriate, given the situation.

I'll illustrate my point with another story from Bob and Hannah.

After their Bible study one day, Hannah asked Bob what his thoughts were on the pains virgins felt when having sex for the first time. Being the expert he thought he was, Bob went on to explain his thoughts in amazing details. They had many conversations of the sort before things became really sorry.

While it was not evil to say those things, it was definitely not appropriate to say them to Hannah, especially given the fact that there were feelings involved with both of them. By constantly discussing things like that with Hannah, he was creating an atmosphere with his mouth, an atmosphere that would burst forth rains when it got full. Let your conversation be always full of grace, seasoned with salt, so that you may know how to answer everyone[g].

Physical Atmosphere

All actions, especially those that affect others, happen on a physical plane. All the actions and things you do not want to do can only get to be done physically. You may have done all the actions in your heart, but the day they happen physically, you know you've lost it. A man may think about sex a lot, but the day he does it, reality dawns on him. The physical atmosphere becomes easy to form when the mental atmosphere and the uttered atmosphere are in place. The more you think about these things, the more difficult it becomes for you to resist when opportunity presents itself. The physical atmosphere is usually a situation or opportunity that makes it almost unavoidable to fall off your wagon. It is the atmosphere where all your senses and the circumstances are working in the same direction. For Bob and Hannah, it was Hannah's room that night. For Becky and Andrew, it was Andrew's room that night, and for Nathan and Lisa, it was the privacy of Lisa's room. Wisdom says to avoid situations that would spark off desires to do evil.

Let me share another painfully true story.

Kingsley was the pastor of his Christian fellowship on campus. He was a firebrand. The members of his fellowship respected him a lot. He even got speaking engagements to speak in churches outside his campus. He was anointed no doubt, but he had a weakness, one he had refused to deal with. He usually spent a lot of his free time dwelling on lewd thoughts and masturbating. He was also addicted to viewing porn. One fateful night, he went out into one of the classrooms on his campus to study. As he studied, there was a lady studying beside him; she had fallen asleep and was resting her head on her books on the table. His thoughts went berserk, and before he knew it, he was fondling her.

When he was sharing this story with me, he was in tears. He never imagined he would find himself in that situation. But the truth is when the physical atmosphere meets with the mental atmosphere, it becomes almost impossible to keep standing. You will inevitably be biting the dust.

The atmosphere you permit would every time determine what you commit.

Check your mental atmosphere. What are the kinds of thoughts you allow into your mind? What are the things you enjoy seeing and hearing? Your mental atmosphere either strengthens your resolve or weakens it.

Check your uttered atmosphere. What are the kinds of words you allow out of your mouth? Do you just allow anything to come out of your mouth, or are you disciplined enough to know what you ought to say to whom and how? Your uttered atmosphere recreates your resolve. It either builds walls around it or chips at it.

Check your physical atmosphere. Are you sensitive enough to notice when the atmosphere favors sin? Are you willing to run off when you know the atmosphere is wrong? Do you purposely create the wrong atmosphere?

Always remember that *the atmosphere you permit would every time determine what you commit.*

Story Time

The Bathroom of Bathsheba![h]

It was springtime. This was usually the time of the year the people celebrated the arrival of new life. The snow was gone with the winter, the grasses were sprouting, the landscapes were showing forth their greenery, and everything looked beautiful. Apart from the trees and the grasses, a lot of mothers were putting to bed. The screams of new babies could be heard from almost every household. It was truly a season of newness. Something interesting about springtime though is that it was also a season where kingdoms sought further expansions; it was the time when kings went to war! The atmosphere at spring was very tense and filled with expectations. That is why Bathsheba felt sad that, year in year out, her expectations were never met.

She was married to Uriah, one of the fiercest soldiers in the king's army. She was the envy of all the other women in the city, for it was an honor to be married to a warrior. She was most fortunate because Uriah was not just a warrior; he was a member of the king's league of extraordinary soldiers. Being a member of that league had its perks. For example, after every war, he usually came home with a large percent of the spoils. His family was also free from paying taxes. Added to that, he was privileged to live in the palace quarters; his home was just two buildings away from the palace walls. Bathsheba had no cause to complain. She had everything she needed; at least that was what the other women thought.

Being a high-ranking military officer, her husband was always away fighting, from one war to the other. She lived with her heart constantly in her mouth. Fridays were terrible days for her; it was the day the personal effects of soldiers that died in war were brought home to their families. The belongings of the soldiers were delivered usually with a letter from the king, stamped with his own signet. It was a letter of honor that brought tears to so many homes. She always stayed indoors, praying and hoping, with her heart pounding as though it wanted to escape from her chest, that Uriah would still be counted among the living. His constant absence was not the only thing that troubled her. She also worried about the fact that they were not building their home. Although they had been married for seven years, they still had no child, and hopes for having children were quickly fading. Their childlessness was not as a result of barrenness or some other health considerations; it was as a result of lack of trying. Every month when she had her menstrual flow, she wept. She wept because she knew that was another opportunity gone with the wind. She wept because she knew that with each flow, hope was moving farther away. According to the customs and traditions of the kingdom, every woman must perform purification rites after each menstrual flow. That was what she was doing, and bemoaning her fate, that fateful evening when it happened.

It was a Friday, and she had as usual locked herself indoors, praying no one came to knock her door with bad news. She had grieved at the wails that were coming from neighbors' houses; she knew that death had visited their homes. After her long wait, she had opened her door to see what was going on outside, but all she saw was sadness. She wept for the families that had lost a brother, a son, a husband, or a father, and wept for herself, for she had gained none. She locked her doors and headed straight for the bathroom to complete her purification rites. Her bathroom was detached from their house; it was a large room built in the middle of the courtyard. Servants were always on hand to do minor tasks like holding out the towels or helping to rub the back of whoever was bathing. The walls were designed with artifacts Uriah had brought home from his many wars. To complete the exquisiteness of the room, the roof was open, giving it a sparkle, as all the gold and silver artifacts reflected the skyline.

As she was washing herself, she got the odd feeling that she was being watched. She quickly moved to grab a towel but changed her mind, allowing fantasies to flood her mind. She let her mind roam. She imagined a tall, handsome man watching her take her bath and coming in to join her, rescuing her from the loneliness she had had to grapple with all her married life. She fantasized on and on, allowing images of a possible future with the imaginary tall and handsome man watching her bathe, a future with many children and lots of love. She was still reveling in her fantasies when one of her maids came to inform her that there was somebody at the door with a message from the king.

Bathsheba hurriedly put her robes on and started toward the door. She knew the inevitable message had finally found her door; it was her turn to mourn her husband. She started to sob as she walked toward the door. A thousand thoughts crossed her mind. She thought about what was going to happen to her without her husband. According to the customs, if a man died without an heir, his brother was to marry his wife to produce children for the man. She wondered if that was going to be her fate. It was a thought like this that sent tremors down her spine, tremors that were seen by the messenger that was waiting outside the door.

The king was tired of fighting wars. "Why do we have to keep with this springtime tradition of bloodshed?" he wondered. The thing about King David was he had had a fair share of wars and battles in his day. As a boy, he single-handedly fought and killed a lion and a bear. As a youth, he killed a huge giant named Goliath. As a young man, he brought the foreskins of two hundred enemy soldiers as a dowry to marry the king's daughter. Now as a king, his kingdom extended to far beyond what an ordinary man could rule over. He was extremely successful. All the neighboring kingdoms were frozen with fear at the mention of his name. But this spring, he just did not feel like going to fight. He sent his soldiers out under the command of his commander-in-chief, Joab Ben Zeruiah. His soldiers marched out, but he remained in the palace adrift in his thoughts.

It had sounded like a good idea to remain in the palace while his soldiers marched out, but now that they were gone, he felt alone. He was used to the action, he enjoyed giving the orders, and he was thrilled by the near-death experiences. Lying on his bed, his mind wandered to victories of the past. He remembered the time when he was almost killed in battle by a giant, the brother of Goliath. He remembered the risks his soldiers had taken for him, and sadly, he remembered how he had wept over the bodies of the ones who never made it out of the battle alive. He thought about the letters he would need to write and sign in the coming days, letters telling families of the loss of their loved ones. As he thought about it, he began to feel uncomfortable, choked by his own thoughts. So he decided to take a stroll along the palace roof to get some fresh air and probably calm his mind.

As he took his stroll, he saw a sight that changed his life forever.

The roof of the palace was flat; it was like a field. The king usually came up to the roof any time he had issues weighing heavy on his heart. The openness of the sky above him had inspired many of his songs and psalms. Usually, he came to the roof looking up and saying, "I will lift up my eyes to the hill from where my help comes. My help comes from the Lord, maker of the heavens and the earth." But on this Friday evening, as he was walking along the roof wall, he was looking down. That was when he caught sight of a woman taking her bath. He had turned sharply away from her direction when it occurred to him that she was beautiful and that he was alone on the roof. He slowly turned around, stealing a look or two from behind his shoulder to be sure no one was watching. And like a boy eating fruits he knew he wasn't supposed to be eating, his mind wandered off. He pictured her looking up to him and beckoning him. Realizing what he was doing, he shook the image off his mind and returned to his chambers.

Now in his room, he fought with his thoughts. He found it hard to shake off the image of the beautiful woman he had just seen. He wondered who she was. Although she looked vaguely familiar, he was too far away to tell for sure, and besides, he did not actually see her face. "Is she married? Is she the daughter of somebody I know?" he thought aloud. After a while, he called one of his servants to find out about her. The servant returned with news David had hoped was wrong. "She is Bathsheba," he said, "the wife of Uriah." King David could see why she had looked so familiar. Now that he knew who she was, his heart was in shreds. The thought of betraying one of his closest warriors tore his heart apart. Worse still was the fact that Uriah was putting his life on the line, while David was sitting in his palace and contemplating sleeping with the man's wife!

King David had his mind made up. He was just going to call her up for a chat; after all, he was bored. He sent messengers to get Bathsheba, while he waited in his room.

"The king calls for your attention" was what greeted her at the door. She did not know what to make of it. Had she done something wrong? Did her husband commit a crime? Was the situation so bad that the king needed to tell her in person? These and a thousand more thoughts ran through her mind. Visibly she was shaken. It was rare to be called into the presence of the greatest king in the entire world. She prayed and hoped for the best as she approached the palace.

Inside the palace, she began heading toward the throne room when the messengers told her she would be seeing the king in his private chambers. Her heart stopped. Suddenly, she understood.

The private chamber of the king was huge. She had never seen anything like it. The walls were high and made of cedar wood plated with gold. The curtains were tapestries of purple and deep-red silk. The room smelled very pleasant, as though there were a furnace of rich fragrance oozing out of it. Bathsheba was taken by what she saw, and much more taken was she by the king's elegance. He was majestic. Seeing him up close was like being next to a god. The king beckoned. With careful steps, she walked toward him, feeling the warmth and embrace of the furry rug under her feet. She sat beside the king on his bed, and then he spoke. All she heard was the sound of many waters; she had gone back into her fantasy. Thoughts of her husband were very far removed from her. All she had fantasized about was right there in that room.

It was two months after that fateful Friday. Even though her fantasies had come true, Bathsheba was torn by guilt. So was David, the king. He had sent gifts and messengers with notes, apologizing for his behavior. They had both agreed to pretend like it had never happened, but that was before Bathsheba noticed that she had not done her purification rites for the last two months. She had not done it, not because she forgot but because she did not have to. Her monthly flow refused to show up, twice! She was pregnant.

What was Bathsheba going to do? She was pregnant for another man while her husband risked his life at the battlefield!

What was David going to do? The wife of one of his most loyal friends was pregnant for him!

A single thought allowed room to roam could ruin your life.

The wrong environment and atmosphere would undoubtedly lead to the wrong action.

The atmosphere you permit would determine what you commit.

Leaving and Cleaving

Scared! That is what a lot of people are. The desire to avoid all the traps and pits that line the road of love has made a lot of people take detours that have led to the wrong destination. A lot of times, people set unrealistic boundaries and pastors and counselors set unrealistic rules. But truth be told, if you are going to have a married life devoid of bitter pills, the road to a solid foundation must be traveled.

Many devout Christian youths have set boundaries to ensure that the period of their courtship does not become a period of sin. As laudable as that is, a lot of them also forget to set the right foundation for the homes they plan to build. You may have gotten scared from reading the previous chapters; you may have even concluded that it was impossible to have a wholesome courtship free from the pitfalls of emotions and untoward actions. You may have even decided on very strict guidelines to help your way through the road that is obviously ridden with twists and turns, but the purpose of this chapter is to quickly remind you that over-carefulness is also as dangerous as carelessness.

Being overly careful makes you keep your eyes on all the dangers that abound on love's journey; it takes your eyes away from the road signs that are meant to direct and guide you. So while one has to be careful, he also needs to understand the essentials of building a relationship. The real reason why many relationships end up in the wrong place is because the people involved did not have a flight plan. So when they got into the air, their relationship kicked into emotion's autopilot mode. They were no longer in control of their travel destination; emotion was. So if the dominant emotion was that of fear of falling into sin and wanton behavior, the journey would be one of over-carefulness. If the dominant emotion happened to be affection and its attending desires, it would be a journey of carelessness. Both journeys would end up at weak and poorly built foundations. That was the problem Berta and Moses had in their relationship. Berta's heart was in a bad place because the guy she had spent months loving did not share her feelings. Moses' heart was also in turmoil because the love of his life had just broken up with him. The combination of Moses and Berta was like a sparky fire. They had no time to plan anything; their emotions were on overdrive. The relationship ended in less than one month.

That is a classic example of carelessness. To avoid these kinds of stories, you need to know the danger points and avoid them; you also need to know how to build a foundation that can support the married life of your dream. I am sure you have gotten the first part down. Now let's talk about your flight plan.

The Basics

Understanding the basics of marriage gives an idea of how to go about it. The challenge most of the time, though, is that people, in their numbers, have mistaken the *wedding* for the *marriage*. So they spend time planning for the wedding, leaving the marriage uncared for in the dark. I have often worried about the increasing rates of divorce and broken courtships. (I hate both.) I have come to find out that they happen because, increasingly, we are becoming more and more vain and shallow; we are building with weaker and weaker foundations. Most people have lost touch with the true meaning and purpose of marriage. I am not going to bore you with all the details of the real meaning and purpose of the sacred union, I am just going to outline the basics so we can shoot off from there.

When God first hinted about marriage, he was planning to make a helper that was suitable for man.[a] That gives us the idea that there was a certain work the man was doing that he needed help with. In other words, marriage is the coming together of two independent people to do a certain work. The million-dollar question then is this: can two people work together except they agree?[h] How do you expect two people from different backgrounds and upbringings, sometimes different cultures, to come together to do one work for the rest of their lives? There would undoubtedly be fireworks! They would have differing opinions and ideas of how it should be done. They would have different time schedules for the work; they would have different lists of whom to call for assistance. They would approach the work in totally different ways. Why? Because they are two totally different people!

But then God again comes to the rescue. He sheds more light on his intention by saying, "Therefore shall a man leave his father and mother and cleave unto his wife."[c] According to God, the result of this cleaving would be oneness! God knew that marriage would be chaos if there was no cleaving! This is where a lot of people have missed it; this is where many foundations went wrong. The courtship and early stages of marriage should be spent ensuring proper cleavage. Many couples spend their courtships either exploring their bodies, giving in to all sort of emotional degradation, or staying away from each other to avoid sin. But let me make it clear here that both foundations are wrong. I call them the double diamond of death. Cleaving, therefore, is the best investment any couple that wants to lead a happy and fulfilled life should give their marriage.

What then is cleaving? What is the process thereof?

To Cleave or Not to Cleave?

Some people call it chemistry, others say it is compatibility, but I prefer to call it the process of cleaving. A lot of marriages have ended with the lame excuse: "We are not compatible." Others have walked out of their marriages shouting into the wind, "I no longer feel the chemistry!" But wait a minute. Why do they realize it after ten years of marriage? Were they blind at the beginning? Obviously, they were too busy swimming in the waters of their emotions to have noticed.

Cleaving is the harmonization of the lives of two people toward a definite goal. So for two people planning to spend the rest of their lives together, they would need to learn *how to live together*; they would need to begin to merge into one. The final result of cleaving would be a new person who is better than each of the former two. They must be ready to leave their old selves and cleave with each other to create a new being. It doesn't mean they forget about what makes them distinct. It simply means they harmonize their differences, forming an alliance for the future.

Cleaving is done in three basic levels. If humans are made up of spirit, soul, and body,[d] then cleaving would need to be done in all three levels.

Cleaving of the Spirit

The spirit of a person is essentially the essence of that person. His faith, hope, and purpose are stirred by his spirit. When two people plan to become one, their spirits need to align. They need to share the same faith, have the same hope for the future, and pursue the same goal and purpose. Many marriages are lopsided. The man is in it for the long haul, but the woman believes divorce is an option. The woman believes in God, but the man thinks God is an option. The man believes in creation, but the woman thinks she evolved from a monkey. Worse still is when the couple believes in God differently. The period of courtship and planning toward marriage should be spent aligning the spirit, because as a married couple, they would need to teach the kids together; they would need to create a whole that has an obvious purpose and direction.

Cleaving of the spirit entails detailed discussion about what is believed and practiced by both parties. It involves studying God's Word together and comparing understanding; it involves having their spirits fed from the same source. It may sound difficult, but it is possible to set a good spiritual foundation for a healthy home.

Cleaving of the Mind

Our plans and ambitions are centered in the mind. The way we achieve those plans also come from the mind. How possible would it be for anything to be achieved if a couple thinks from the opposite end of the room? How can a man who sees a glass as half full succeed with a wife who sees it half empty? For marriage to be successful and goals achieved, the couple needs to see the same picture. True, the perspective may be different, but it should be toward the same direction. A man should be able to discuss at length with his wife any issues that interest him, and so should the woman. Imagine a professor of languages married to a professor of physics. Except for there being a cleaving of the mind, there would be absolutely nothing to sustain the home.

During courtship, a sincere desire to get to know and understand the interests of your partner is of utmost importance. You can read and exchange books, listen to the same music, watch same movies, and do anything that makes your mind go in the same direction.

Cleaving in the Physical

When the emotion begins to wear off in marriage and you find you no longer feel like having sex every day, would you still be able to live together happily? Would you enjoy just being together? If you spend your courtship having sex, you may not be able to find out. Without the sex, can you have fun? What are the things you would enjoy doing together? It is not okay to sit back doing nothing and say, "After all, we are not sleeping together." Do something. Take up a project together, work on an idea, plan a business, do something, anything, that tasks your minds and creates tension. See how you cope with the stress and tension generated by the both of you; learn how to handle each other. Do something to improve how you *work* together.

When you spend time together like this, pursuing cleaving, you would find that you are in charge of the affairs of your courtship. You are in the driver seat, navigating toward the married life you dreamed about.

Take responsibility. Don't let emotions lead.

Love: *Pure and White*

Many young girls dream of a castle with a window where she sits and sings to the birds, waiting for her Prince Charming to come and take her away. As she grows up, her castle becomes an office and the window becomes heavy traffic. Her song is the sound of her computer keyboard typing away, and the birds are files of work to do. She discovers that her prince was not so charming after all. She sighs and says, "Well, this is life."

The story of disappointed expectations is so common today. People get married with high hopes, only to find out a few years down the line that they are battling for the custody of the kids. Where did all the promise of love disappear to? Where did all the sweet sensations vanish to? What happened to all the butterflies in your tummy? You may say life happened, but I beg to differ.

A lot of people wake up angry because of the person sleeping beside them. They find that they are attracted to somebody at the office. The husband finds his wife less and less attractive, and the wife finds her husband more and more annoying. The circle continues, and then one day they are both staring at divorce papers! What happened to all the excitement at the beginning of their life? Where did all the love go? You may say it went with time, but I beg to differ.

At the beginning of marriage, couples enjoy spending time together. They go on trips and vacations. The wife can't wait for her husband to return from work. The husband keeps looking at his wristwatch, hoping it will soon be time for him to get off work. Two days away from each other feels like two years. They Skype, they chat, they "ping," they do everything to stay in touch. But a few years down the line, the wife really doesn't care what time her husband returns home. In fact, she appreciates the peace and quiet. The husband prefers to do long hours at work. He doesn't mind that his wife was still asleep when he left home in the morning. Their life becomes a routine. What happened to the joy of being married? What happened to their spontaneity? You may say they got busy with life, but I beg to differ.

The truth is people let the effectiveness of their love wane, and so with time things begin to get complicated. The fact that we *are in love* doesn't just automatically make things okay. Like communication, we need to love effectively. It is our act of loving that makes the marriage solid after many years of flood and fire.

Love being a verb is an act we should keep doing. We are not in love because we say it; we are because we do it. At the beginning of every relationship and marriage, we find it easy to *do* love because the feelings and emotions are still very active. But with the passing of time, we begin to get weary in the *deed* of love. That's where many marriages begin to head south. Like we have previously established, love is different from emotions, and so the feelings of emotion are not good tools in the measurement of love. Love is measured by how much you do to make your mate feel loved. We hear of ministers of God going through dirty and shameful divorce. It is usually not because they cheated on their spouses or because they did unholy things; it is usually because they get so involved in their ministry that they forget they had vowed to "have and to hold, to love and to cherish." They stopped *doing* love and started living through the motions. In courtship, we find out what makes our partners tick. We discover what moves them to tears; we see what makes them feel loved. In marriage, we begin to do those things, until we get tired. But just imagine that after being married for forty years, you still care about those little thoughtful things. Love is not meant to stop after a while, it is meant to continue for life.

Truth be told, living together as a couple brings to light a lot of things that make it difficult to love, but like we established earlier, learn to *make* the decision to love. Usually, we let the emotions of anger and bitterness, disappointment and hurt, control the way we act. But like earlier said, leading emotions are the bane of successful marriages and homes.

To be able to love effectively, it is important to set the foundation right. Apart from cleaving, there are some things that need to be done. It is wisdom to always do the first things first.

First Things First

Being humans that we are, sentiments, emotions, and feelings control our decisions. We order things based on how we feel per time. What we refuse to realize is that the order and perspective from which we view life and things matters a great deal! In our love relationships and marriages, it would be of utmost value that we put things in place in the right order; it is immensely important that we see things from the right perspective. A deep look at the opening words of the Bible and the first things God did as he created the world gives us a clear understanding of what important values we need to build into our marriages, especially at the beginning.

The first name recorded in Scriptures is God![a] God is the beginning of all things. In our love relationships and marriages, the most important name, the most important personality, the first person on the acknowledgment list, is God. You see, we read a lot of books and listen to a lot of speakers and attend a lot of seminars and then conclude we have gotten it all figured out. We go around hitting our chests, boasting to all and sundry that we have just the right formula for a successful marriage. Yet it is God who works in you to will and to act according to his good purpose.[b] Every relationship and marriage built with God as foundation will be able to stand through the days of sunshine and rainfall alike.

The first verb (action) recorded in Scripture is *create.*[a] Many times, our relationships and marriages die not because the Devil threw ballistic missiles at them but because we refused to be creative. At creation, God imparted unto us his creative ability. So we are expected to create life, fun, love, joy, peace, excitement, a God-glorifying environment, and all the things you can mentally picture into our relationships. The act of creating is the most important thing to learn. Create new ways of doing things. This is the rest of your life we are talking about. Chances are it is going to get boring living with one person. Therefore, create new ways of doing everything.

The first place recorded in Scripture is *heaven!*[a] Wow! How often do we miss this? How often do we place so much emphasis on ourselves, our dreams, and our marriages? But from here, we can see that the most important place our love and even our marriages should focus on is heaven. Amidst all the fun and excitement of marriage, we are still to "seek first the kingdom of God …."[c] So if my relationship is not focusing on heaven, there is already something wrong with the foundation. If marital life becomes so demanding that it takes me away from focusing on heaven, I have begun to skid down hell's path. So ask yourself this: has my relationship drawn me closer to heaven? Is my marriage leading me to heaven's gate?

The first recorded state of the earth was *shapelessness and chaos!*[d] Have you not wondered why all the talk of peace seems to be bringing more trouble? It is simply because the default state of the earth is chaos. Now this somehow translates into our love life. Although we are in love, we cannot help but have issues. The news that fills the air is that of failed marriages, homeless children, single parents, etc. Many times, this chaotic mess destroys the beautiful and blossoming love and sends us down the path of fear. This situation can be brought under control, but only when the ingredients are right. It is those ingredients we have been talking about. Putting things in place according to the right order solves the problem of chaos. If my relationship or marriage has God as a first, has creativity deeply entrenched, and has heaven as focus, it will be encapsulated from the default chaos present on the earth.

The first force of influence recorded in Scripture is *the spirit of God!*[d] Wow! This is a serious pointer to what the most important force influencing our lives and love and relationship and marriage should be. We talked about the chaotic state of affairs on earth. To solve it, God did not call a board meeting; He just allowed his Spirit to *brood over it.* If we would allow God's spirit to brood over our love life, then chaos would be a forgotten issue. Many couples take the issues that bother their marriages and make them public affairs. People at their office know what goes on at home and their in-laws are called to settle the problems. Even worse, some couples drag themselves to court. What influences your relationship? What gives direction to your marriage? You or God's Spirit?

The first thing God did was *to speak*[e]*!* Wow! He did not call an executive meeting; he did not brainstorm; he did not debate. He just spoke. Can you remember the first words you spoke to your loved one? What kind of words do you speak generally? God knew the importance and power of the spoken word. He said, "Death and life are in the power of the tongue ..."[f] God used this power to create life. So what do you use your tongue for? What kinds of words do you say? A husband complains about his wife's attitude and says all sorts of evil words to her. What he doesn't know is that he is inevitably shaping her with his words. Like Jesus does for his church, every man should do for his wife, to make her holy, cleansing her by the washing with water through the Word.[g] Instead of complaining, he builds her up; she builds him up with blessed words.

God is also in this passage, pointing out the power of speaking in the morning (figuratively). Speak life into your relationship from the beginning; speak life into your marriage from the start; speak life to your kids from their conception; speak life from the crack of dawn; speak, just speak. Just be sure you are speaking life.

The first thing God created was *light.*[e] Have you ever wondered why He created light first? It is because He needed his workspace lighted up. Many people have their relationships and marriages shrouded in thick darkness. From the very start, there is the darkness of lies and deceit and secrets and all sorts of pretentious hypocrisy. Light up your workspace. Set off your relationship on a lighted workspace. From the beginning, let out all the cats from the bag: no more secrets, no pretence. Get rid of all surprises that may spring up later in the marriage, say all that needs to be said, and light up the workspace. When you are working in the full view of light, you'll be able to quickly detect anomalies and correct them. In the light, your focus and destination would be so obvious that you cannot fail. One of the essential *firsts* in your relationship should be light. Lighten up your workspace!

The first expression of God we see in Scriptures is that of thankful joy.[h] "And God was pleased with it …" One would wonder who God was smiling at, who he was thanking! He was thanking himself, appreciating what he had done. It is essential to be appreciative in our love relationships. A simple "Thank you," or a simple, sincere "That was a nice job," is all you need to bring out the joyful spark in your mate. You know, along the way, we usually begin to expect our mates to do some things. We take them as duties. But gratefulness is like grease applied to wheels to overcome the inevitable friction. Just like God, let's make a thankful attitude one of our firsts.

Notice that God did all the firsts on the first day. That is why the remaining five days of creation went totally hitch free. Do you want a hitch-free marital life? Then do the first things first!

Love Gives Room to Grow

In Genesis, the Bible tell us that God made Adam go into a deep sleep and then took a rib from his side to make Eve.[i] That is a story that has sparked a lot of controversy. Many people have even dismissed it as fiction. But the truth is there are a lot of lessons we can glean from that story.

From the story, Eve started out as a bloody mess of a bone. That was all there was to her. I am certain that if Adam had seen her in the bloody state, he would have decided to have nothing to do with her. But Adam slept till she became his pride and joy. That is the case with many couples today. They get excited about the idea of love, but along the line, Mr. Adam notices that Mrs. Eve is not as perfect as he had hoped. The next thing that happens takes place in a courtroom. But love, real love, gives room to grow. Imagine how Adam looked after the bone had been taken out. I am certain he would have been out of shape and messed up with blood patches all over. What would Eve have done if she saw him like that? But the Bible says God went on to close the flesh from where he had taken the bone.

Like our first parents, we all have something in us that needs fixing; we have lingering baggage from our pasts that tend to interfere with our present lives. Those things do not just disappear with the advent of love. What love does is creating an environment that engenders growth. But what do we see today? We see wives nagging at their husbands; we see husbands getting violent. We see couples taking it out on each other in one way or the other. But real love creates an atmosphere for change; it gives time for the messy bone to become beautiful, elegant Eve; it realizes that with time and the right environment, Adam's messed-up side would be healed. Sometimes we look out for the mess in our partner's life without realizing there is also a mess in our lives we need to sort out. It takes a good deal of patience and understanding to let the flaws heal, but if you are in love as you claim to be, you wouldn't mind the wait.

Story Time

A Tale of the Lonely Midwife[j]

Everybody was in a panic; this child was taking too long to be born. Its mother had been laboring to bring forth the child for two days straight. It seemed death was inevitable. The little family community was in silence, hoping and praying that evil news would not greet them. They had been like this for the past two days. At first, they gathered to celebrate, and then they began to worry. Now they were past worrying; they were praying for the worst to be averted.

It was dusk, and the sun was setting just over the horizon. The little children were asleep from boredom, and the animals were locked up in their pens. The women were gathered around the house where she was, and the men were sitting in groups of twos and threes, discussing the probable cause of the delay. Inside the house, the woman was quiet; she was tired from exertions. Even the midwife had lost ideas as to what to do. Everyone had lost hope; some people were even beginning to retire to their houses. That was when it happened; that was when the shrill first cry of a baby filled the air. Like a thirsty man who just found water, the little community burst into life. The cry of the baby was soon dulled by the shouts of joy that filled the air. Everybody was alive again. Even the little children had woken from their sleep and were joining in the celebration though they had no idea what was going on.

The entire family community gathered in front of the house where the miracle had just happened. They were eagerly waiting to see the miracle and the miracle worker. As was the custom, the midwife came out with the baby, lifted it up, and said, "Let's welcome our new member." The small crowd cheered and jumped around with glee, hugging and congratulating me. The midwife scanned through the crowd as though looking for somebody. Her face lit up when she saw him leaning on a pole away from the crowd, smiling at her. She immediately handed the baby over to me, its father, and ran joyfully toward her smiling husband. The stress and hard work of the past two days seemed so distant; her husband's smile was the only thing in her current world! The midwife was the wife of my uncle.

The thing about Abram and Sarai was that they played and flirted with each other as though they were still teens. Looking at Sarai, nobody would believe that she was sixty-five years old already. She still looked strong, agile, and beautiful. Her main sorrow was the fact that even though she was the family's midwife, and had helped all the women deliver their babies, she still had none of her own. Nobody could rival her midwifery skills, but she still heard the gossips and she still felt the lingering gaze of people any time she went out into the town. She had done everything she could—taken every drug, made all the demanded sacrifices, visited the best physicians of the time—but nothing worked. She had endured the pains; she had endured the gossips, and she had endured the loneliness. Worst of the things she had to endure was the endless complaining of some neighbors. For example, after the last delivery, she heard me complain bitterly about the fact that I had gotten yet another female child. I had even threatened to marry another wife. This just got Sarai all worked up. She found herself crying, wondering why people who had children had anything to complain about. That was not all; there was the threat from her husband's brother.

Abram was the first of three sons. His youngest brother died really early, but not before having a son to take over his estate. Nahor, Abram's other brother, also got married and had children, a lot of them sons. You see, sons were very important to these men. That was why when Abram, their eldest brother, still had no *child*, they decided to act fast. Nahor called together the elders of the family to rule on his brother's case. According to him, anything could happen any day to anyone. Citing the example of their youngest brother, he believed a man should be ready at all times. The elders concluded that Abram should marry another wife.

Abram knew it himself; he needed to do something. He was heavily disturbed. He had worked hard to become wealthy. He was the wealthiest man in the family. He usually found himself wondering what use the wealth was if there was nobody to bequeath it to. Like Sarai, he had done every necessary thing to get a child, but nothing had worked. He had also had to endure the whispers and secret jests. Worst of it all, he had suffered through the endless tears of his wife. Any time there was a delivery, he always prepped himself, because he knew that night would be a tearful one. What was he to do? He loved his wife, but he needed an heir.

Life was exciting for them when they just got married. Their expectations were high. Being wealthy, Abram planned to have a lot of children. But as the years passed, the silence grew, and the excitement died. The only comfort they had was in their love, and what love it was.

The love between the two of them was so strong. Sarai called Abram lord. That was because he bore all her burdens. He was there to dry her tears after the delivery sessions; he was there to console and comfort her from the pains inflicted by the gossips, and he was her backbone. I did not know how much he loved her until the day after my baby was born.

Sarai had come to my home to check on my wife. She had come to help bathe the baby when she heard me complain to my friends that I was tired of having female children and that I wanted another wife. I saw her drop the things she was holding and dart out the door with her face buried in her hands. I knew I had hurt her. She ran home, straight to the arms of her husband. I had immediately run after her to apologize. When I got to her house, I saw her on her knees before her husband, asking him to marry another wife. She wanted him to put an end to all the noise and gossip her childlessness was causing. I stood by the door, eavesdropping. The reply of my uncle shocked me. He stood up from the chair he was sitting in, lifted up his wife, and said, "I married you not because I wanted children, but because I wanted you! Eleazar, my servant, would be my heir."

What a lesson on love! I have learned that love doesn't wane with challenges but grows stronger. I have learned that love sticks it out through the cold and heat. Even though the people in love grow old, love never grows old.

Finding Peace with God

Irene was embittered. She did not know what to do. She would not have believed even if a prophet had told her she would do what she did. She had believed it, preached it, counseled other young people about it, but now she had become a victim of her messages. More than just a victim, she had also lost the ability to hide. For the past three months, life had been hell for her. She had had sex with her fiancée and was now pregnant. She felt God was punishing her because she had sex. What was she to do? The disgrace was too much for her to bear, but much more than the disgrace was what she had done to God. How could she have let herself slide? She couldn't pray, she couldn't study her Bible, and she couldn't face the disgrace that came with the pregnancy. She could see it on the faces of the people she had once preached to; it was obvious that this was never going away. What was she to do? How was she to get her life back? Could she ever be the Christian she once was?

Cynthia was devastated. She had led a reckless life in the past. The shadow of the past kept looming all over her. She desired to be free from it, but somehow a voice kept telling her she was going to reap all she had sown. Even though she wanted to be married as a virgin, she had gone on to sleep with men beyond counting. Now she was afraid she wouldn't find a good man for a husband. She had since repented of her ways, but the sights and sounds still filtered into her mind. What was she to do? Was God still angry with her?

Agnes was a very devout Christian. She lived every day as though she would be called up to heaven soon. She was dedicated and committed to her Lord. But one day, in the heat of passion, she had let a fellow Christian brother feel her up. She was devastated. She wept profusely and prayed fervently to her Lord for mercy and forgiveness. She had made a mistake. Was she to suffer for it? Two years into her marriage, she still finds herself shedding tears; she still looks back with regret, wishing it never happened.

Life is full of mistakes. We all have bitter stories of the past, especially those that filter into the future. Making mistakes, taking the wrong turn, has been part of human history. But God gives hope to them who seek it.

The Lie

The fear of the repercussion of actions is a force that drives many people. From the day of the mistake, they begin a future of fear. Some people have been so tormented in fear that instead of turning away from the evil, they throw up their hands in despair and say, "Well, the deed has already been done." They just keep going deeper and deeper in the sin. That was the case with Cynthia in the opening chapter. Immediately she broke her vow to wait until she was married before sex; she got entangled in a web of fear. The fear pulled her deeper and deeper into sexual sin, so deep that she was even sleeping with her uncle!

Guilt is another emotion that tears people apart. A lot of people are torn in pieces by the guilt they feel from the sin they had fallen in. They live the rest of their lives regretting and beating up themselves. Satan keeps whispering in their ears, reminding them of how much they have fallen. He differentiates the holiness of God from their sinfulness and tells them there is no more hope.

The most annoying thing is that church people are responsible tools in the hands of Satan. They come, Bible in hand, condemning and casting out, making you feel there is no more hope. But truth be told, there is hope.

It is true that you sinned; it is true that the action may affect the rest of your life. It is true that you have caused yourself some pain; it is also true that God still cares! This point was emphasized by the life of a young lady. Rita had fallen in love with Tim and was having the time of her life. They were together for about two years. Like many young people, they couldn't control the fire of passion that had built up in them, and after a while, Rita got pregnant. She was devastated: she was pregnant, and she was twenty! What was she to do? Added to the pains, Tim had also started to act strangely. He no longer cared for her. She had to endure the pain, shame, ridicule, confusion, and, worse still, a broken heart! Tim left her in the midst of the pregnancy. She hated the world, hated God, hated Tim, and hated the baby. She called it the mistake of her life. It is at this point that a lot of young people throw caution to the wind. Rita did not.

The Truth

The moment you realize you're wrong and turn to God for mercy, you start a journey into a new life, a life of freedom and deliverance, a life where your slate is clean before God. He said if we confess our sins, he is faithful and just and will forgive us our sins and purify us from all unrighteousness.[a] Remember the story of the woman that was caught in adultery and brought to Jesus?[b] She was condemned to be stoned by the religious leaders. The problem with many people is that they go to the wrong people when they fall from grace. Many people run to their leaders for absolution. While there is nothing wrong with going to religious leaders, there is everything wrong with making them the first port of call. The sin was against God, who is the one with the power and wherewithal to absolve you of it. The woman's problem started because before Jesus, she had met with the religious leaders. But thank God for Jesus. He said, "Then neither do I condemn you. Go now and leave your life of sin."[c]

That is the same message Jesus is giving today. As long as you come to him, he is ready to absolve you. All he expects from you is a promise not to return to the sin. Satan's winning ace is guilt. He rattles your heart with guilt so your eyes are blinded with tears and you can't see the way forward. But the Bible says, "There is now no condemnation for those who are in Christ Jesus because through Christ Jesus the law of the Spirit who gives life has set you free from the law of sin and death."[d]

The realization of these truths makes you reengineer your mind. It was true that you sinned, but it was also true that you repented of them. It is true that you have been forgiven; it is also true that your slate has been wiped clean because "anyone united with the Messiah gets a fresh start, is created new. The old life is gone; a new life burgeons."[e] Don't let Satan cheat you into doubts and fear and guilt. Reengineer your mind into accepting what Christ had done for you, and embrace the peace that he gives because "embracing what God does for you is the best thing you can do for him."[f]

What about the Scars?

As I write this section, I am drawn to a huge scar on my right hand. I still remember vividly the events that led to the scar. It was so painful at the time it happened, I felt I had been disfigured for life. A lot of us have scars in one area of our life or another. These scars don't go away.

We made the wrong decision, and there is always that baby to remind us of it. We made the wrong turn along the road, and there is always the wasted time to remind us of it.

But do you know your scars can become stars? Do you know your mess can become a message? God can take that painful experience and bring glory out of it. He took Rahab, the harlot, and made her an ancestor in the line of salvation. He took Ruth, an outcast, and made a virtuous woman out of her. He took Bathsheba, the cheating wife, and made the fruit of her womb glorious. He took Moses, a murderer and made him into a savior. He took Saul, a serial killer, and made him into a great Apostle. He can take your *history* and make it into *his story* of your life. When you turn your past over to him, he makes it beautiful. "That's why we can be so sure that every detail in our lives of love for God is worked into something good".[g]

This was the understanding that helped Rita out of her guilt-ridden life. She braced up and pursued a life of loving God. She gave birth to Michael, a wonderful boy who has become the joy of her world. She spends her time today telling young people like her how to avoid the same mistakes she made.

Cynthia was also not left out. She got this understanding and followed after her Lord. Today, she is pursuing the call of God on her to make more and more young people enter a covenant of abstinence. I can remember the broad smile on her face the day she got the first person to make that covenant with her. Her mess had become her message!

What about the scars? Hand them over to him. He specializes in making them into stars.

<u>Story Time</u>

The Confessions of a Sinful Man!^h

I was shaking all over. The tremors were moving rapidly down my spine. I did not know what to make of the whole situation. The postman, without a word, handed me the mail. I knew what the content would be, and I wished I would be disappointed. The mail was not in the conventional envelope. It was a papyrus rolled into a rod and tied with a thread. It looked like it had been dispatched in a hurry. As soon as the letter landed on my hands, I felt the cold shiver, the type associated with death, running down my spine. My palms became sweaty, and my knees began to gently knock against each other. I knew this was it. I knew the deed had been done, and I knew it was never going away!

I dispatched the postman with an odd smile and quickly dashed to my inner chamber. I was afraid the reality of the news the letter was carrying would send me south; I did not want anybody to see me in such a state of paralysis. Inside my room, I carefully untied the red rope that had been used to tie the papyrus. As I untied it, I wondered about the color of the rope. Was it really red? Or was it stained with blood. Once or twice, out of anxiety, the letter dropped out of my hands. My heart was racing as I finally took off the straps and began to gently open the letter. I could literally hear my heart pounding as I read out the last sentence of the letter: "And he is dead"! I sank onto my bed in despair. Alas, one of my most loyal and trusted friends was dead—killed by my orders!

The thing you should know about me is this: I am not a cold-blooded killer. Truth be told, I have been a soldier all my life, and I have enjoyed killing enemies, but that is where I draw the line. Outside the battlefield, I am the kindest and nicest person around. I dedicated my life to helping the helpless. My home was constantly besieged by people who needed hope, people who needed justice, people who at one time or the other had been ignored and neglected. I spent my days attending to them and meeting their needs. Apart from being a super philanthropist, I was also very emotional with God. I loved him with very deep passion. It did not matter what people said about me; all that mattered was worship. There was this one time I organized a festival in honor of God. I was so excited that I danced, truly danced, in the streets till I was almost naked. I remember my wife complaining, telling me that my behavior was inappropriate. You see, I was the king.

The deed I had done, as was represented in the letter, was a sharp contrast of who I really was and who I genuinely wanted to be. I could not even believe I stooped low, using my power to wreak havoc not just on anybody, but on my own friend and ally! Looking back to the day the whole mess started, I feel bags of tears weighing down my eyes.

Like many sad tales, it started with a woman.

It had started about two months ago. How I regret the decision I took not to join my comrades in the tradition of the time. You see, it was the time when kings went to war. I had stayed home, idling around when I saw her bathing. I should have turned away, but I let my gaze linger. Instantly, I knew I wanted her. That was the beginning of the mess I found myself in.

I was told she was the wife of one of my most trusted warriors. I remembered her husband, Uriah. He was a brave man. He had fought by my side countless times. He was by my side even when my boss, the king before me, declared me an outcast and was hunting for my head. Uriah was a man of honor that deserved to be treated with honor. So dedicated and mighty was he that he was named amongst the top thirty soldiers in the empire. Despite these facts, despite the fact that I knew he was presently away and fighting to defend my kingdom, I went ahead and slept with his wife. It was like I was controlled by a monstrous demon. I couldn't help myself. I couldn't stop myself.

After that fateful evening of evil fun, my conscience broke. My heart hibernated. I felt like a man who swallowed a rock. I was ridden with guilt. It became worse when a few days ago she told me she was pregnant by me! I invited her husband back from the war and tried to make him go sleep with his wife so it would appear like he was responsible for the pregnancy, but honorable Uriah would not go home to his wife. He said he couldn't spend his time having fun in his wife's embrace while his compatriots were spending their time in death's embrace on the battlefield. That was the point at which I felt a bitter seed take root in my heart. I knew he was right, but I chose to be angry at him for making me feel so filthy and mundane. I hated him for reminding me of the incontrovertible truth. After rebuffing my attempts to make him sleep with his wife twice, my mind was made up. I told him to prepare to head back to battle in the morning. I was planning to spend the night perfecting my plan.

Though I thought it was going to be fun, that night was terrible. Everything screamed out to me, telling me to stop. I took my royal pen and sat at my table to write. As I put the pen to ink, I immediately remembered that this was the same position I had always taken whenever I was moved to write a psalm of worship to God. It was the same table I wrote on, the same chair I sat on, and the same pen I wrote with. The difference here, though, was that I was not writing a psalm of worship but the death warrant of an innocent man, a better man! My tears flowed freely as I wrote. Uriah was to deliver the letter that would send him to the afterlife; he was to be the carrier of his own death!

I sinned against Uriah! I slept with his wife, got her pregnant, and killed him! What a mess I created. I tried to make peace with my conscience by marrying his wife, but that complicated things the more because every time I saw her, I remembered my evil. It became worse when the prophet Nathan came to denounce my actions, claiming that

God was extremely angry with me. What was I to do? There was nobody I could turn to. I had sinned against myself; I had sinned against my friend. I had sinned against God! I couldn't forgive myself. I knew my friend couldn't forgive me from the grave. I knew nobody would forgive me. I even doubted God's ability to forgive me. What was I to do? Was this the end of me?

It was in the midst of this confusion I decided. It was in the midst of this turmoil I made my mind up. It was better to fall into the hands of the living God than to fall into the hands of men. It was better to attempt to seek God's forgiveness than to wallow in guilt. I remembered some of the psalms I had written about God's mercy. I knew that he gets angry once in a while, but across a lifetime, there is only love. I knew that if I turned to him, the nights of crying my eyes out would give way to days of laughter. So I lifted my voice up to the only one who could redeem me. I took up the pen of my iniquity, sat on the chair of my sins, and wrote on the table of my transgression. I composed my prayer in tears, saying it out loud as I wrote.

> *Thus went my prayer:*
>
> *Generous in love—God, give grace! Huge in mercy—wipe out my bad record.*
> *Scrub away my guilt; soak out my sins in your laundry.*
> *I know how bad I've been; my sins are staring me down.*
> *You're the One I've violated, and you've seen it all, seen the full extent of my evil.*
> *You have all the facts before you; whatever you decide about me is fair.*
> *I've been out of step with you for a long time, in the wrong since before I was born.*
> *What you're after is truth from the inside out. Enter me, then; conceive a new, true life.*

*Soak me in your laundry and I'll come out clean, scrub me
and I'll have a snow-white life.*
*Tune me in to foot-tapping songs, set these once-broken bones
to dancing.*
*Don't look too close for blemishes; give me a clean bill of
health.*
*God, make a fresh start in me, shape a Genesis week from the
chaos of my life.*
*Don't throw me out with the trash, or fail to breathe holiness
in me.*
Bring me back from gravy exile; put a fresh wind in my sails!
*Give me a job teaching rebels your ways so the lost can find
their way home.*
*Commute my death sentence, God, my salvation God, and
I'll sing anthems to your life-giving ways.*
Unbutton my lips, dear God; I'll let loose with your praise.
*Going through the motions doesn't please you; a flawless
performance is nothing to you.*
I learned God-worship when my pride was shattered.
*Heart-shattered lives ready for love don't for a moment escape
God's notice.*[i]

And true to my prayer, he noticed! He noticed my heart break,
noticed my repentance, and noticed my tears. He came to my rescue
and forgave my sins. I still had to face some of the consequences of my
actions, but I got my life back! The prophet Nathan came with most
cheering news. He said God had decided to make a dynasty out of my
kingdom. My sons after me and their sons after them would reign on
the throne as kings.

What an honor to have a God to run to! What a joy! What a
privilege!

Endnotes

Milling the Mile

a. John 8:32 (KJV).

Wow! I'm in Love!

a. "Natural Attraction or Lust? Vertical Thought." United Church of God. http://www.ucg.org/marriage-and-family/natural-attraction-or-lust, accessed June 19, 2012.

b. "Infatuation or Love?" http://www.ucgstpaul.org/lit/gn/gn067/youth67.htm, accessed June 19, 2012.

c. National Geographic (2006), "Love: The Chemical Reaction." http://ngm.nationalgeographic.com/ngm/0602/feature2/index.html.

d. John 3:16 (KJV).

e. "Infatuation or Love?" http://www.ucgstpaul.org/lit/gn/gn067/youth67.htm, accessed June 19, 2012.

f. Gal. 5:22.

g. 1 Cor. 13:4–7 (MSG).

h. "On Things That Matter: The 12 Tests of Love." Chip Ingram. http://www.onthingsthatmatter.com/inspirations/the-12-tests-of-love-by-chip-ingram, accessed June 19, 2012.

i. Story is adapted from Judges 4 and 5.

Bonds: Electrovalent or Covalent
a.   1 John 4:18 (NIV)
b.   Story is adapted from Genesis 34.

The Day Wise King Solomon Got Confused
a.   1 Kings 3:12 (NKJV).
b.   Prov. 30:18 (MSG).
c.   Prov. 30:19 (MSG).
d.   Prov. 30:19 (NASB).
e.   Prov. 30:19 (GW).
f.   Prov. 30:19 (GNT).
g.   Prov. 30:19 (TLB).
h.   Story is adapted from Judges 13-16.

Energy in Motion
a.   Prov. 30:18.
b.   Gen. 25:21–34.
c.   Gen. 25:21–34.
d.   Matt 1:18-20.
e.   The story is adapted from 2 Samuel 13.

The Atmosphere You Permit
a.   1 Thess. 5:22 (KJV).
b.   Prov. 4:23 (MSG).
c.   Job 31:1 (MSG).
d.   Prov. 23:7 (AMP).
e.   Phil. 4:8 (MSG).
f.   Luke 6:45 (MSG).
g.   Col. 4:5 (NIV).
h.   Story is adapted from 2 Sam 11.

Leaving and Cleaving

a. Gen. 2:18.

b. Amos 3:3.

c. Gen. 2:24 (KJV).

d. 1 Thess. 5:23.

Love: Pure and White

a. Gen. 1:1.

b. Phil. 2:13 (NIV).

c. Matt. 6:33 (KJV).

d. Gen. 1:2.

e. Gen. 1:3.

f. Prov. 18:21 (KJV).

g. Eph. 5:26 (NIV).

h. Gen. 1:4.

i. Gen. 2:21, 22.

j. Story is adapted from Genesis 12 and 15.

Finding Peace with God

a. 1 John 1:19 (NIV).

b. John 8:1–11.

c. John 8:11 (NIV).

d. Rom. 8:1, 2 (NIV).

e. 2 Cor. 5:17 (MSG).

f. Rom. 12:1 (MSG).

g. Rom. 8:28 (MSG).

h. Story is adapted from 2 Samuel 11 and 12 and Psalm 51.

i. Psalm 51:1–17 (MSG).